Thistle Versus Rose

Scotland, England and 700 Years of Love, Hatred and Indifference

'All the English care about it money. Ask a Scotsman for directions and he'll tell you which way to go; ask an Englishman and he'll try to sell you a map.'

It's 700 years since the Scots thrashed the English at Bannockburn. Has there ever been a better opportunity to celebrate seven centuries of winding up the English?

Exploring everything from money, diet, war and weather to language, love and landscape, *Thistle Vs Rose* is a hilarious miscellany of Anglo-Scots rivalry. Introduced by Susan Morrison, it features quotes, jokes and trivia from Robert Burns, Billy Connolly, Frankie Boyle, Robert Louis Stevenson and many, many others.

Susan Morrison

Thistle Versus Rose

Scotland, England and 700 Years of Love, Hatred and Indifference

SCEPTRE

First published in Great Britain in 2014 by Sceptre
An imprint of Hodder & Stoughton
An Hachette UK company

First published in paperback in 2014

1

A CIP catalogue record for this title is available from the British Library

ISBN 978 1 473 60501 5

Typeset by Palimpsest Book Production Ltd, Falkirk, Stirlingshire

Printed and bound by Clays Ltd, St Ives plc

Hodder & Stoughton policy is to use papers that are natural, renewable
and recyclable products and made from wood grown in sustainable forests.
The logging and manufacturing processes are expected to conform to the
environmental regulations of the country of origin.

Hodder & Stoughton Ltd
338 Euston Road
London NW1 3BH
www.hodder.co.uk

Contents

Introduction

Two Scotsmen were cast ashore on a desert island. Three years later a rescue team discovered them and found they'd built three churches. Why three, the rescuers asked, when there are only two of you? 'Well,' said one. 'He attends that church, I attend that church, but neither of us will be caught dead in *that* church.'

This is the beauty of the Scot. Two men struggling for survival against unimaginable adversity, who get to know each other so well they can fall out over a matter of theology and yet still cooperate enough to build a place of worship each, plus one they can jointly denounce and spurn. These are the brilliant, inquisitive, visionary intellects that gave the world penicillin, pneumatic tyres and waterproof rain-wear, and still found time to generate the entire user guide for Western thought out of the powerhouse known as the Scottish Enlightenment. 'We look to Scotland for all our ideas of civilisation', observed Voltaire. John Amyatt, an English chemist, said of our capital city in the eighteenth century, 'Here I stand, at what is called the Cross of Edinburgh, and can, in a few minutes, take 50 men of genius and learning by the hand.' Even one of England's greatest heroes, Winston Churchill, asserted that 'perhaps only the ancient Greeks surpass the Scots in their contribution to mankind'. The Scots: a nation of thinkers, talkers and doers.

Two Englishmen were cast ashore on a desert island. Three years later the rescue team found them. They hadn't spoken to each other since first being washed up on the beach. Asked why not, the shipwrecked mariners explained that they 'hadn't been introduced'.

Of course, had an Englishman and a Scot been washed up together, the rescue team would have found a British Embassy with the Englishman installed as Ambassador and a fully functioning hydropower system created by a Scotsman who was just showing off. They still wouldn't be speaking to each other, mind.

You English like to think that you annoy us. You don't. You amuse us. You let yourselves be run by a cabal of nanny-raised finalists for Upper-Class Twit of the Year, who endlessly denounce the nanny state for trying to keep the peasants alive by passing laws preventing decent members of the land-owning classes sending workers into mines and up chimneys without hard hats on. Political correctness gone mad, I tell you.

You baffle us. You have a bizarre, fawning attitude to royal people, which is weird given that England once held the title of Most Revolutionary Country, World Heavy-weight Division, 1649–60, when the international stage rang to the thud of Cromwell's riding boots and his backing band, the New Model Army. Long before Soviets and communes, you tried and executed a king. You declared a republic. You raised the flag of representative democracy. And then thought better of the whole thing, dug out the king you happened to have in reserve and began centuries of toadying to royal people on the grounds that 'they bring in the tourists, you know'.

Don't get me wrong, we're quite keen on the Queen

up here, and enjoy a sneaky admiration for that gaff-prone fella of hers. He's like that embarrassing uncle most Scots have, who downs five pints of lager at the family wedding and then makes inappropriate, mildly racist comments about the waiting staff on the grounds that 'they don't look British'. In fact, they are all from Birmingham and are studying for PhDs in advanced nuclear physics.

Incidentally, said dead king was technically OUR king, on account of him being a Stuart and all, and we graciously allowed his father, James VI, to accept the proffered throne of England when your Queen Elizabeth turned out to be as useless at breeding as a giant panda – but we'll overlook that.*

You perplex us. You don't like foreign food on holiday, but you eat curry at home. You say sorry all the time. If an alien abducted a Scot and threw him unknowing into a strange city, the best advice I can give – and believe it or not, people are always asking me, 'Susan, what should I do if I get dropped by aliens into a strange city?' – would be to stomp on someone's foot. If THEY apologise, you're in England.

You infuriate us by endlessly referring every international football game back to some game in 1966 against Germany. It's not like we endlessly rumble on about Sir Chris Hoy, Andy Murray and the 2002 Winter Olympics women's curling team.

Dear old Vera Lynn sang 'There'll always be an

---

* And we won't mention that you also managed to decapitate his granny, Mary, Queen of Scots. Jesus, you lot have form with the Stuarts . . .

England', but where is it? What is it? Like Narnia, Shangri-La or Lilliput, it's a place we all know the name of, but can never actually find. Even one of your prime ministers, Sir John Major, a man so violently dull even his own reflection can barely muster the enthusiasm to materialise, tried to sum up 'England' in terms of a sort of Bertie Wooster theme park. Warm beer, he said. Cricket on the green, and spinsters bicycling to evensong. So that's it? A place that serves substandard beverages while watching a game they get thrashed at by foreigners? And as for that spinster, well, as any fan of *Inspector Morse* will tell you, she is a sexually frustrated volcano who's been stalking the vicar for years and she's got the bloody head of the last man who scorned her advances in her bicycle basket.

The truth of the matter is that 'The English' don't exist. We have to plunge far into the land beyond the Tweed before we can find someone who actually describes themselves as 'English'. Scousers would curl their lip in disdain. Geordies are set apart by an accent as impenetrable and lyrical as Gaelic. Yorkshire and Lancashire are too busy re-fighting the Wars of the Roses, and revel in soft southern bastards being scared of them. Even further south, the Cornish prefer to wrap themselves in an atmospheric fug of Uther Pendragon, Round Table Knights and psychopathic smugglers.

Why 'The English' should be surprised by Scotland's sudden desire for independence is a complete mystery to us since, increasingly, England is starting to look like a nervous chap standing on a rapidly disappearing ice floe.

It's the oldest and arguably most successful union of two nations in European history, but still Scotia seems to yearn for a place of our own. Sadly, you seem to have no idea why we want to take out a separate mortgage. You're just standing there with your cardigan done up wrong, egg on your tie and the *Daily Mail* slipping from your nerveless fingers. Behind you, Jeremy Clarkson stares mutely from the television screen, while you endlessly intone 'Why, darling?'

We're not all bravado and swagger though. We worry too. Who will look after you when we leave? Will you remember to take your tablets? Can you be trusted to go on holiday yourself and not piss off the locals? Will there be honey still for tea? Because Nanny might forget to buy it.

There will always be an England. We just don't know where it is. Or what it is. But we think we can help. To start with, it isn't us. And are we rivals? No, that would not be fair, but we let you think that. Why do we let you think that? Well, silly, because that way everyone thinks of you as the big bad guy, but everyone loves the plucky little Scot. It's been that way for seven centuries, in every sphere of life, and there's never been a better time to laugh about it. Along the way we'll see what history's great and good have observed about Anglo–Scots rivalry (sorry, *relations*). Come on, let me show you how we did it . . .

Susan Morrison, Scotland

I

Deep Fried What? *Food and Drink*

We live on the cold, rainy edge of the world. Not for us sunny slopes to grow grapes and olives, or the warmth to cultivate the oranges, limes or lemons of a Mediterranean orchard.

For us, it's oats.

Mind you, given the short straw there with the crop choice, we make them work for their money. You might know oats only as a breakfast dish, but up here we stuff poultry with them, roll soft cheese in them, make them into wee biscuits that you can have with that soft cheese, and to top it all off pour the stuff into drawers, let it cool and turn it into a handy (if not terribly hygienic) snack that can be enjoyed for days, sometimes weeks. So versatile is our national cereal that it can also serve as a dessert! Forget about the 'mighty' English puddings – sponges, roly-poly, and steamed floury nonsense involving jam – and savour instead that unrivalled delight, the flapjack. There's really nothing the humble oat can't do. In an emergency you can even use it as a face pack. Try doing *that* with spotted dick and see where it gets you.

In the nineteenth century, oats took a bit of an elbow when whisky (from the Gaelic uisge-beatha, meaning 'Water of Life') became the after-dinner tipple of the English upper classes and barley was the new thing to grow. The English discovered our national beverage through Sir Walter Scott, Scotland's first tourist officer, who made everything Scottish fashionable. By 1822, King George IV was even asking for Glenlivet by name during his state visit to Scotland – even though it wasn't strictly legal at the time. Parliament passed the Excise Act in 1832 to make distilling legal and, of course, taxable. We relentlessly improved the process to create ever better whisky, and then in 1880 God joined in and sent the phylloxera bug to decimate the vineyards. No wine, no brandy. Hello, international export markets.

Whisky went on to conquer the world and pass itself off as the national drink of Scotland, with bottles swathed in tartan and wee white dogs doing the adverts. Fair enough. Whisky is, indeed, a Highland drink. It was not the alcoholic beverage of choice for the lowlander. For centuries, believe it or not, we lowlanders drank wine – oceans of the stuff. The Port of Leith was home to a massive import industry of burgundies, clarets, champagne – you name it, we knocked it back. In fact, so much French plonk came through Leith in the eighteenth century that a mathematician worked out that every Scot – man, woman and child – was putting away a pint and half of the stuff *a day*.

Getting reeking drunk was not the social faux pas it's considered to be today. You got yourself into less trouble, for one thing (no cars to drive, remember). And at dinner, a cheery bloke would go round loosening your neckerchief, lest you accidently hanged yourself by slumping in your chair. The great and the good were at it as well. Our legal eagles, for example, felt they operated much better under the influence. Lord Newton considered himself a far superior judge when he'd hit his daily optimum operating alcohol levels of six bottles of claret.

Scotland, then, was a nation merry on drink. But we didn't realise we had our own ticking time bomb in the drinks cabinet. Back in 1680 James, Duke of York and brother to Charles II, was sent north to impress the Scots. And how was he to do that? Well, the English had taken to this newfangled tea thing with huge enthusiasm over the previous couple of decades. So James headed over the border with a caddy of the stuff to feed to the nation that drank claret for breakfast.

Tea was proffered. The Scots drank. They liked. They liked a lot.

The English just used tea as an excuse for a sit-down. Not us, no sir. For us it was fuel to drive a revolution. Scots do everything with a messianic zeal, you see – 'Look! We've given up the bevy and taken to the brew, and so could you!' It was perhaps the greatest U-turn in modern history. We loved this new-found sobriety, and went on to create a whole movement out of it: temperance was born. We were good at it, and spent much of the Victorian era exporting the notion to the Americans who, being Americans, took the whole thing too far and went from abstinence to prohibition and opened the door to organised crime. Thus, drinking tea at the Palace of Holyrood House in 1680 led to the Volstead Act in 1919 and the rise of Al Capone.

Sobriety, my friends, is overrated.

That other great Scottish vice, sugar, met temperance, and Irn-Bru was born, a drink the same colour as a freshly fake-tanned Essex girl and with a chemical composition kept secret to this day. Anyone can drink Irn-Bru, but it takes a Scot to enjoy it. Our southern neighbours could only come up with dandelion and burdock – which, let's face it, has an image problem with the name, right there. It's a sad brown slurry with no claims to cure hangovers and it's a pushover for the multinational monsters of Coke and Pepsi, whereas our bright orange contender consistently knocks the Yanks off the number one beverage spot – in Scotland, at any rate.

Oats. A grain, which in England is generally given to horses, but in Scotland supports the people.

Samuel Johnson

I once saw an English guy in Glasgow trying to order a pint of lager and lime and the barman went: 'We don't do cocktails.'

Frankie Boyle

Freedom an' whisky gang thegither.

Robert Burns

Only in Scotland does the guy in front of you in McDonald's order a double cheeseburger, triple fries, and a *diet* Coke.

Ian Black, *Scotland vs England*

Here we are, progressing tenfold, buying the right bread, real croissants, we're making fresh muesli and we understand what a great cup of coffee is. And then some idiot brings out a deep-fried chocolate sandwich.

Gordon Ramsay

The proper drinking of Scotch whisky is more than indulgence; it is a toast to civilisation, a tribute to the continuity of culture, a manifesto of man's determination to use the resources of nature to refresh mind and body and enjoy to the full the sense with which he has been endowed.

David Daiches, *Scotch Whisky*

A double Scotch is about the size of a small Scotch before the War, and a single Scotch is nothing more than a dirty glass.

Lord Dundee

The majority of Glasgow pubs are for connoisseurs of the morose, for those who relish the element of degradation in all boozing . . . It is the old story of those who prefer hard-centre chocolates to soft, storm to sunshine, sour to sweet. True Scots always prefer the former of these opposites.

Hugh MacDiarmid,
The Dour Drinkers of Glasgow (1952)

Love makes the world go round? Not at all. Whisky makes it go round twice as fast.

Compton Mackenzie, *Whisky Galore!*

A good gulp of whisky at bedtime – it's not scientific but it helps.

Sir Alexander Fleming (1881–1955),
discoverer of penicillin, on his cure for a cold.

Never drink whisky with water and never drink water without whisky.

Scottish proverb

Patient: If I give up drink, tobacco and sex will I live longer?
Doctor: No, it'll only seem like it.

Chic Murray

A favourite eighteenth-century Scottish toast was to 'the little gentleman in black velvet' – the mole whose hill caused English King William to fall off his horse and die.

What butter and whisky will not cure, there is no cure for.

Scottish proverb

My theory is that all of Scottish cuisine is based on a dare.

Mike Myers

The Recipe for Haggis, 1826
MEG DODS
From Rosemary Goring's Scotland: The Autobiography

Sheep's pluck [lights, liver and heart] and paunch, beef-suet, onions, oatmeal, pepper, salt, cayenne, lemon or vinegar.

Clean a sheep's pluck thoroughly. Make incisions in the heart and liver to allow the blood to flow out, and parboil the whole, letting the windpipe lie over the side of the pot to permit the discharge of impurities; the water may be changed after a few minutes' boiling for fresh water. A half-hour's boiling will be sufficient; but throw back the half of the liver, and part of the lights, trimming away all the skins and black-looking parts and mince them together. Mince also a pound of good beef-suet and four or more onions. Grate the other half of the liver. Have a dozen of small onions peeled and scalded in two waters to mix with this mince. Have ready some finely ground oatmeal, toasted slowly before the fire for hours, till it is of a light brown colour and perfectly dry. Less than two teacupfuls of meal will do for this quantity of meat. Spread the mince on a board and strew the meat lightly over it, with a high seasoning of pepper, salt, and a little cayenne, first well mixed. Have a haggis bag (i.e. a sheep's paunch) perfectly clean, and see that there be no thin part in it, else your labour will be lost by its bursting.

Some cooks use two bags, one as an outer case. Put in the meat with a half-pint of good beef gravy, or as much strong broth as will make it a very thick stew. Be careful not to fill the bag too full, but allow the meat room to swell; add the juice of a lemon or a little good vinegar; press out the air and sew up the bag, prick it with a large needle when it first swells in the pot to prevent bursting; let it boil slowly for three hours if large.

2
Legal Tender: Money

The Scots have an unfair reputation for being tight-fisted with their hard-earned cash. It's said that the music-hall Scot Sir Harry Lauder paid for everything by cheque, hoping that the lucky recipient would be so chuffed to have an autograph from the great man that they would never cash it. Of course, this stereotypical meanness has its advantages, particularly to the waiters and taxi drivers of foreign climes, who find that the average Scot on holiday has an unexpected tendency to tip like a roaring-drunk *Rockefeller*. We hurl currency about in a desperate attempt to lay Lauder's ghost to rest, especially if there's an Englishman present. We're not mean, you see – we're haunted. We've been broke before.

The Darien Scheme was a bad idea that broke a nation.

Scotland wanted a colony, like her big English neighbour. Colonies, the reasoning went, were good for business, and Scotland in the seventeenth century had had a fairly torrid time of it, what with religious wars, upheaval and the next-door neighbours having a civil war (which actually started in Edinburgh) that just made life difficult for everyone. Oh, and the weather changed as well, meaning famine was the order of the day.

So, in the early 1690s, a ball of fire called William Paterson managed to persuade the Scots to invest in the Darien Scheme, to be built on the Isthmus of Panama.

With hindsight, and Google Earth, we can survey his earthly paradise and tactfully point out a whole host of heartaches, but Paterson was a man with a plan. Even worse, he was a Scotsman with a plan – a force to be reckoned with if ever there was one. And to top it all, this Scotsman had already founded the Bank of England.

Our colony would bedrock a mercantile empire to rival the Dutch, who hoovered up the world's wealth and spent it on tulips. This appealed to the near-bankrupt Scots (the wealth, that is, not the tulips. We leave that sort of thing to foppish Bloomsbury types). We promptly started to hand over our cash. You can get an idea of how much we fired across by the size of the money chests used by the Company of Scotland Trading to Africa. There's one at the National Museum of Scotland. In all, we raised £400,000 (£44 *million* today) – not bad for a country down on its luck.

We should have put the lot on a horse: the scheme was a disaster. A regular witches' brew of bad planning, bad luck and bad neighbours. We didn't fully understand where we were going, we took the wrong people and goods, and the big boys already out there, the Spanish and the English, didn't want us joining the party so didn't lift a finger to help. Of the 3,000 or so original would-be colonists, only a few hundred ever saw Scotland again. William Paterson survived, but his wife and son did not.

The result was an economic catastrophe for Scotland, and probably led to the Union Of Parliaments. And we all know where that's got us. Even more disastrously, the penniless Scot became a bit of a fixture in the English psyche.

Take a look at old Hogarth's *Gate of Calais* (1748). It's about the English eating good roast beef while the French look on, mouths a-dribble. Essentially, it's a swipe at the French, but what's this slumped in the shadows in the foreground? Why, a starving tartan-clad spectre. A Highlander, probably a fugitive Jacobite. Hogarth didn't like the Scots (to be fair, he didn't like anyone), but it says a lot about the hard times we'd found ourselves in.

The Scots might have been penniless once, then, but they did eventually crack the secrets to running nations' finances – probably because they knew the impact of getting it wrong. Adam Smith from Kirkcaldy dismantled entire economies and put them back together to see how they worked, and created the beast we now call an economist.

Smart lad he might have been, but he was also reckoned to be the most boring man in Edinburgh. He talked to himself a lot. And at parties he'd get a load of wine down his neck and face the wall. To be honest, that seems to be an economist's idea of a wild night out.

Margaret Thatcher, it was said, carried a copy of his masterwork *The Wealth of Nations* in her handbag. French politicians, relentlessly sideswiped by Madame Thatcher's loaded reticule, were doubtless unaware that the penniless Scot from the 'Gate of Calais' was getting his revenge . . .

All the English care about is money. Ask a Scot for directions and they'll tell you how to get to where you want to go; ask an English person and they'll try to sell you a map.

Anonymous

How many Scots does it take to change a light bulb? Och, it's no' that dark . . .

My parents used to take me to the pet department and tell me it was a zoo.

Billy Connolly

The English are worried about the euro being brought in because of loss of national identity and rising prices. In Scotland, people are just worried in case they have to close Poundstretcher.

Frankie Boyle

Jock and Jimmy were walking along a street in London.

Jock looked in one of the shop windows and saw a sign that caught his eye.

The sign read, 'Suits £5.00 each, Shirts £2.00 each, trousers £2.50 per pair'.

Jock said to his pal, 'Look at the prices! We could buy a whole lot of these and when we get back to Scotland we could make a fortune. Now when we go in you stay quiet, OK? Let me do all the talking 'cause if they hear our accents, they might think we are cheap Scotsmen and try to screw us. I'll put on my best London accent.'

'OK Jock, I'll keep me mouth shut,' said Jimmy.

They went in and Jock said in a posh voice, 'Hello my good man. I'll take fifty suits at £5.00 each, one hundred shirts at £2.00 each and fifty pairs of trousers at £2.50 each. I'll back up me truck ready to load them on, old chap!'

The owner of the shop said quietly, 'You're from Scotland, aren't you?'

'Well yes,' said a surprised Jock. 'What gave it away?'

'This is a dry-cleaner's.'

A deaf Scotsman will hear tha clink o' money.

Scottish proverb

Our business in this world is not to succeed, but to continue to fail in good spirits.

Robert Louis Stevenson

There are few more impressive sights in the world than a Scotsman on the make.

J. M. Barrie

Two Scots bet a pound on who could stay under water the longest. They both drowned.

Anonymous

The copper wire was invented when two Scots were fighting over a penny.

Billy Connolly

3
Gees a Shot o' yer Tutu: Culture

The Scots have always regarded culture as interactive – just ask any English comedian. We call it 'banter'. They call it 'heckling'.

Glasgow in particular used to have a fearsome reputation for eating English comedians alive. Indeed, the city's Empire Theatre was notorious within showbiz circles as 'The English Comic's Grave'. Brothers Mike and Bernie Winters were one of many Sassenach acts subjected to a barrage of banter at the hands of the second house audience one evening during the peak of their popularity in the early 60s. Or Mike was, at least – Bernie was still to make his appearance. When Bernie joined his brother on the stage he was greeted with stunned silence, until a voice roared from the dark, 'Aw fuck. There's two of them.'

Mind you, Mrs Winters' boys got off lightly. Heckling flattened Des O'Connor, who fainted on stage. They say the exaltation from the crowd sounded like the Zulu victory roar at Isandlwana.

Glasgow may have perfected weapons-grade heckling, but Dundee invented it. The Tayside city was known for three things in its heyday – jam, jute and journalism – and it was the second of these that gave us heckling. Jute, you see, was how you made rope. In the nineteenth century the process involved tearing out the heckle, a nasty fibrous mass embedded in the raw jute. It was truly dreadful stuff, which ripped the skin off the worker's hands. The people who carried out this job were called hecklers. And they were among the first workers to create organisations resembling early unions.

Occasionally, mill owners sent lackeys round to inform the workforce that meal breaks had been binned, therefore workers would have to eat their own left legs. But some of the workers were ready, willing and organised enough to shout them down – the hecklers, who passed their wisdom down through the ages to ensure that English comedians learned a thing or two about Scottish sensibilities.

Of course, comedy is a low art, I suppose. If asked to name one of the 'high arts', many of us would not hesitate to suggest poetry, 'The record of the best and happiest moments of the happiest and best minds', as Shelley described it; that noble art form that 'makes immortal all that is best and most beautiful in the world'.

But not us. For us, it's never been that soppy. In 1504, William Dunbar and Walter Kennedy, esteemed court poets to James IV, held a flyting, where two poets, live and before their king, insult each other in glorious, soaring verse. The language is utterly magnificent. Kennedy accuses Dunbar of being a short ugly dwarf who writes crap, and Dunbar hits back by calling Kennedy a hideous walking corpse who leaks shit. It's also the first time the word 'fuck' ever appears in print. Oh, and we also invented rap at the same time.

James's lechy southern neighbour, Henry VIII, was livid. The flyting had been a huge hit, but poor old Henry didn't have one court poet, let alone two, who were capable of this standard of rhyme, metaphor and foul language.

In a rage he picked on one poor bugger, commanding him and another bloke to write a flyting.

It was rubbish. We can't even find it. And isn't it therefore tempting to imagine the Scottish ambassador sitting through the first poet and then, when the second would-be flyter lurches on, muttering under his breath, 'Aw fuck, there's two of them!'?

Later English poets were wont to do a bit of wafting in the Lake District, apparently being startled by daffodils (what did they think would see? Raptors?). Our poets, by contrast, were muscular chaps who could plough the 100 acres, sow the winter wheat, shoe a carthorse, impregnate two wenches, translate a dirty poem by Ovid from Latin, drink every man in the pub under the table and still knock out a love poem before bedtime.

Today, the Scottish love of interaction, drink and poetry combine every year in the ultimate poetry and dance slam, the Burns Supper. Robert Burns is the world's greatest poet, and a man resolutely unsurprised by daffodils. His birthday is celebrated every year on 25 January. Haggis is stabbed, whisky is drunk, songs are sung, but best of all: we, the Scots, dance.

Scottish country dancing is not for the faint-hearted. For one thing, it's more of a contact sport than a cultural expression. Imagine an entire line of American football quarterbacks heading straight for you, but wearing kilts. People are picked up, hurled about and thrown against the walls, to the accompaniment of accordion music and wild war cries. Everyone has a great time, even the ones who wind up in casualty.

There is no equivalent down south. There is an English tradition of Morris dancing, but to use the Scottish expression, 'This place is so boring you could start a riot with a balloon on a stick.' That, my friends, is Morris dancing. With bells on.

Of all the small nations of this earth, perhaps only the ancient Greeks surpass the Scots in their contribution to mankind.

Winston Churchill

I was going through a town called Bathgate at around 11 o'clock at night. And there was a guy leaning and pissing against a front door. He then took out his keys and went inside.

Frankie Boyle on 'the most Scottish thing I've ever seen.'

We look to Scotland for all our ideas of civilisation.

Voltaire

Unpleasant, unfair, cruel and above all smug . . . the lumpy and louty, coarse, unsubtle, beady-eyed beefy-bummed herd of England.

A. A. Gill on the English

Whaur's yer Wuillie Shakespeare noo?

Overexcited theatregoer at the first night of John Home's play *Douglas*, December 1756

What we, the Scots, do is stoicism with an air of disgruntlement. That is our failsafe coping mechanism. We're good at it.

Gary Sutherland, journalist and author

It is not real work unless you would rather be doing something else.

J. M. Barrie

I don't know why I should have to learn algebra. I'm never likely to go there.

Billy Connolly

A Scots pessimist is a man who feels badly when he feels good for fear he'll feel worse when he feels better.

Scottish proverb

When shall I see Scotland again? Never shall I forget the happy days I passed there, amidst odious smells, barbarian sounds, bad suppers, excellent hearts, and most enlightened and cultivated understanding.

Sydney Smith

Did not strong connections draw me elsewhere, I believe Scotland would be the country I should choose to end my days in.

Benjamin Franklin

When I came into Scotland I knew well enough what I was to expect from my enemies, but I little foresaw what I met with from my friends.

Prince Charles Edward Stuart (1720–88), letter, quoted in Blaikie, *Itinerary of Prince Charles Stuart* (1897)

The Scots are not at home unless they are abroad.

George Orwell, *The Lion and the Unicorn*

It is never difficult to distinguish between a Scotsman with a grievance and a ray of sunshine.

P. G. Wodehouse, *Wodehouse at Work* (1961)

If thy neighbour offend thee, give each of his children bagpipes.

Anonymous

In their food, clothing, and in the whole of their domestic economy, they adhere to ancient parsimony . . . They delight in variegated garments, especially striped, and their favourite colours are purple and blue . . . In their houses, also they lie upon the ground; strewing fern, or heath, on the floor, with the roots downward and the leaves turned up . . . They have all, not only the greatest contempt for pillows, or blankets, but, in general, an affectation of uncultivated roughness and hardiwood, so that when choice or necessity induces them to travel in other countries, they throw aside the pillows, and blankets of their hosts, and wrapping themselves round their own plaids, thus go to sleep, afraid lest these barbarian luxuries, as they term them, should contaminate their native simple hardiness.

George Buchan, *The Habits of Highlanders* (1582)

The average Englishman, in the home he calls his castle, slips into his national costume – a shabby raincoat, patented by chemist Charles Mackintosh from Glasgow, Scotland. En route to his office he strides across the English lane, surfaced by John Macadam of Ayr, Scotland. He drives an English car fitted with tyres, invented by John Boyd Dunlop of Dreghorn, Scotland.

At the office he receives the mail bearing adhesive stamps invented by James Chalmers of Dundee, Scotland. During the day he uses the telephone invented by Alexander Graham Bell, born in Edinburgh, Scotland. At home in the evening his daughter pedals her bicycle, invented by Kirkpatrick Macmillan, a blacksmith from Dumfries, Scotland. He watches the news on TV, an invention of John Logie Baird of Helensburgh, Scotland, and hears an item about the US navy, founded by John Paul Jones of Kirkbean, Scotland. He has now been reminded too much of Scotland and in desperation he picks up the Bible, only to find that the first man mentioned in the good book is a Scot – King James VI, who authorised its translation.

Nowhere can an Englishman turn to escape the ingenuity of the Scots. He could take to drink, but the Scots make the best in the world. He could take a rifle and end it all but the breech-loading rifle was invented by Captain Patrick Ferguson of Pitfours, Scotland. If he escaped death, he could find himself injected with penicillin, discovered by Alexander Fleming of Darvel, Scotland, and given an anaesthetic, discovered by Sir James Young Simpson of Bathgate, Scotland. Out of the anaesthetic he would find no comfort in learning that he was as safe as the Bank of England, founded by William Paterson of Dumfries, Scotland.

Ian Black, Scotland vs England

4
Who Runs this Place? War and Empire

Bannockburn should have been a warning to the rest of the world: this is what happens when the Scots get their act together. We are unstoppable.

In 1314, the Scots readied themselves for battle. Robert the Bruce was match-fit and ready for a fight with Edward II, who wasn't half the fighting general his cantankerous old man had been.

The curtain-raiser was a spectacular Spielberg moment: the Bruce himself was surprised, while riding alone, by a group of armoured English knights led by Henry de Bohun. The Bruce hadn't donned any armour yet, and was armed with only a battleaxe. De Bohun lowered his lance and spurred his huge warhorse forward. The Bruce stood firm on his little palfrey. De Bohun thundered towards him. At the very last second, Robert the Bruce rose in his stirrups, dodged the lance and buried his battleaxe in Henry de Bohun's skull in an exploding welter of blood, brains and English eyeballs*. It went downhill for the English from that moment on, until Ed fled the field.

Of course, not all Anglo–Scots battles went so smoothly. In 1513, at Flodden, James IV faced an army raised by

---

* Sorry to be so graphic there, just thought the occasion called for it.

his own sister-in-law and headed up by a man who really knew his business, the Earl of Surrey. That didn't go so well. James got hacked to bits on the battlefield, the last British monarch to meet his maker in this way.

Eventually, of course, the wars between the Scots and the English stopped, mainly because of the joint-throne-sharing initiative of James I & VI after the Act of Union in 1603. There was the occasional encounter: Dunbar, Pinkie Heugh, Culloden. But then we got our hands on their Empire. And the English got their mitts on the Scottish soldier – a very useful thing to build an empire with . . .

When it came to the Empire, the Scots took a practical view. They quickly realised that the English didn't really have a clue beyond teaching the natives how to play cricket, which apparently made up for being colonised. The Scots liked this for two reasons: one, it kept the English public-school boys busy until they went home or died of fever, whichever came first; and two, cricket is not a Scottish sport, so we're not interested in playing it, but we're thrilled when former colonies thrash the bejeezus out of England, even if we don't understand what's just happened.

It was said that the English acquired the Empire in a fit of absent-mindedness, which suited the Scots right down to the ground. If they hadn't even noticed getting an empire, why, they wouldn't notice who was running it. The Scots became the imperial middle management.

Now and again we acquired other bits and pieces to add to it – Hong Kong, for example, thanks to two enter-prising Scots, William Jardine and James Matheson, who bumped into each other in a Chinese brothel in the 1830s. Our bold boys started to trade: tea to Britain and opium to China. Two vices with one stroke.

The Chinese weren't too keen on the opium side of the business, and finally banned it altogether, which didn't suit our lads, who viewed this as an infringement of their liberties. So, egged on by the Jardine and Matheson double act, the Empire roused itself and made for China, to defend the rights of a pair of drug dealers.

We took big stuff like battleships and Congreve rockets against bannermen and wooden war junks. It was an imperial smackdown. China lost. But on the bright side, namely ours, a treaty set the opium traders free and we got Hong Kong.

The Empire's greatest drug barons became rich beyond the dreams of any street-corner hustler. Jardine bought a townhouse in London, a castle in Perth and a seat in the Commons. Matheson bought the entire Isle of Lewis. No man is an island, but some can afford to buy them.

Victoria's armies advanced across the globe until the sun could never set on her Empire (good thing too – who would trust an Englishman in the dark?). However, the roll-call of generals who led those battalions had names like Campbell, Cochrane, Elphinstone, McDonald and Napier. The viceroys, diplomats and civil servants boasted surnames such as Elgin, Moray and Melville.

We didn't need to fight you to get your Empire, England – we just snuck it away. You hardly even noticed . . .

To characterise the English as evil colonialists is to ignore the fact that the Scots pretty much ran the Empire for us, with great enthusiasm and efficiency.

Tim Lott

It's nae good blamin it oan the English fir colonising us. Ah don't hate the English. They're just wankers. We are colonised by wankers. We can't even pick a decent, vibrant, healthy culture to be colonised by. No. We're ruled by effete arseholes. What does that make us? The lowest of the fuckin low, tha's what, the scum of the earth. The most wretched, servile, miserable, pathetic trash that was ever shat intae creation. Ah don't hate the English. They just git oan wi the shite thuv goat. Ah hate the Scots.'

Renton in Irvine Welsh's *Trainspotting*

A plane is shot down over Iraq and Saddam Hussain captures a Scotsman, an Englishman and an Australian. Saddam says, 'I'm not as cruel as George Bush says I am. You will be given fifty lashes each but you can have whatever you want on your back.'

The Australian goes first and asks for the finest kangaroo hide there is to cover his back. This is granted and he receives the kangaroo hide before he receives fifty lashes. His back is all torn and bleeding but he survives.

The Englishman shouts defiantly, 'I will take it as it comes; I will have nothing on my back and will be proud to bear the scars. Stiff upper lip you know, eh what.' His wish is granted and he receives his fifty lashes, his back torn and bleeding, his ribs fractured and protruding, a terrible mess to behold.

'Now Jock, it's your turn – you have the same choice as the other two. What would you like on your back?' says Saddam.

Jock replies quickly and without hesitation: 'I'll have the Englishman.'

It is not for glory, nor riches, nor honours that we are fighting but for freedom – for there alone, which honest man gives up but life itself.

> The Declaration of Arbroath, Scotland's 1320
> 'Declaration of Independence'

I believe passionately in English independence.

> Alex Salmond on *Newsnight*, 10 January 2007

Forty-eight Scottish kings buried in this tumbled graveyard – before the Norman conquest of England in 1066. And today should a man be bold enough to refer to the Scottish nation, he is looked upon as a bit of a crank.

> Neil Gunn on Iona, *Off in a Boat* (1938)

It has suffered in the past, and is suffering now, from too much England.

> A. G. Macdonnell (1895–1941), *My Scotland*

Since the time of Alexander III, the Stone of Scone, known popularly as the Stone of Destiny, had played a symbolic role in the assumption of royal power. It was removed from Scone Abbey in Perthshire by Edward

I's men in 1296 and placed in Westminster Abbey, where it became a focus for nationalist resentment. Many dreamed of returning it to its rightful place at Arbroath Abbey. With due ceremony it was finally returned to Scotland in 1966, but a valiant and briefly successful attempt was made early on Christmas Day in 1950 by Ian Hamilton and three fellow students, as Hamilton recalls here:

The Stone should now theoretically have slipped out, but it was a very close fit and its weight made it unwieldy . . . I seized one of the iron rings, and pulled strongly. It came easily – too easily for its weight, and I felt something uncanny had happened. 'Stop!' I said and shone my torch.

I shall not forget what the faint light revealed, for I had pulled a section of the Stone away from the main part, and it lay in terrifying separation from its parent.

I was going to be sick. Everything was now turned to a new purpose which was not good. Better to howl and bring the watchman and have it repaired than carry away a broken Stone.

'We've broken Scotland's luck,' came Alan's awful whisper.

Rosemary Goring, *Scotland: the Autobiography* (2007)

Mary Queen of Scotland arrived, a widow, with two galleys, from France . . . At her arrival the sky itself plainly told what comfort she brought for this country, namely sorrow, pain, darkness, and all impiety. For, in living memory, the skies were never darker than at her arrival, which for two days thereafter continued like that; for, besides the excessive wet, and the foulness of the air, the mist was so thick and so dark that no man could another much see beyond the length of two pairs of boots. The sun was not seen to shine two days before, nor two days after. God gave us that warning; but, alas, most were blind.

John Knox, *History of the Reformation in Scotland* (1559–66)

5
You and Whose Army? Heroes

In Scotland, we can be heroes. But just for one day. The next day, we'll make sure you're cut right back down to size. Heroism is just showing off. It's not the sort of thing a Scot is bred up to aspire to. The English, now, they have a clear procedure for worshipping heroes and what to do with them. It's all cheering crowds, adoring women, pop up to the Palace, bob down on one knee, tap on the shoulder and knighthoods all round. I think it's something to do with the Knights of the Round Table. The English think anyone with a Sir in their name has to be a hero, even if they find out later they've been selling secrets to the Soviets.

No sooner does a Scot become a hero than another Scot is ready to cut him (or her) down to size. Now, there is a reason for that. We're a small country and we all know each other, or at least we think we know each other. That means that there's a strong chance we might know the great hero's family and so be privy to the secrets of his shady past. It's difficult to accept an MBE when someone behind you mutters 'I remember batterin' that wee sod for copying my homework.' Everything in Scotland is known.

Few nations, however, have ever blended heroism and failure with such panache as Scotland.

I give you Bonnie Prince Charlie or, to use his full

name, Charles Edward Louis John Casimir Sylvester Severino Maria (yes, Maria) Stuart. He's usually to be found on the front of a shortbread tin. The man is a marvel of marketing and has undoubtedly done sterling service to Scotland's baked-goods industry. He must shift an Everest of the stuff every year. He's impossibly romantic – because he failed.

It all started well. Women swooned over this perfumed, powdered and kilted gallant as he marched down from the Highlands, kicked the arse of the only government army in Scotland at Prestonpans, stopped for a bit of a party in Edinburgh, then on into England, where George II was apparently having a fit of the vapours and ready to hightail it back to Hanover. BPC got as far as Derby, thought better of it, headed for home, got thrashed at Culloden and then became the stuff of legend by going on the run through the Highlands to eventually escape to France and then Italy, where he became a truly Scottish hero by drinking himself to death. Starts off well. Goes downhill fast. Late recovery at the end. That's a Scottish hero.

John Paul Jones had a textbook heroic Scottish career. Born in Kirkcudbrightshire in 1747, he became known as 'Father Of the American Navy'. His belligerent career took him to the American War of Independence where, with his French warship *Bon Homme Richard*, he got up to all sorts of mischief. He attacked Leith, and then got jumped by three Royal Navy ships, who proceeded to batter him to a pulp. The Captain of HMS *Serapis* asked Jones if he wished to surrender – this was just about the point that the bow of the American ship was slipping below the waves – but Jones came back with a one-liner worthy of Bond: 'Sirs, I have not yet begun to fight.' John Paul Jones somehow got on board the *Serapis*, fought the crew to a standstill, seized the 22-gun warship and took it back to America. Big hero. Everybody loves him. So, in true Scots fashion, he falls out with the Americans, lights out for Imperial Russia, persuades Catherine the Great to give him a ship, falls out with the Russians and winds up in Paris, where he dies broke. And then, in a final chapter, the Yanks remember the old 'Father of the American Navy' bit, find his remains in 1906 and take him back to a hero's welcome in America. They can identify him, they say, because the French took the precaution of pickling him in alcohol.

You see? That's why we don't trust the showy ones. True Scottish heroes have changed the world, but you probably don't realise it. You'll have seen them. In virtually every medical and scientific documentary, there they are, the quietly spoken man or woman with degrees coming out of their ears, earnestly explaining why they've spent the last twenty-five years of their lives staring down a microscope or looking up a telescope.

They are the descendants of people who looked at mouldy yuck and thought, 'That might cure something.' The folk who wired up bits and pieces to create televisions and telephones and fax machines, or came up with different ways to think about economics, geology or philosophy.

Shy, unassuming and retiring, that's how we like our heroes. Peter Higgs is not Scots by birth, but being Scots isn't a nationality, it's a state of mind. And he proved his qualification for being Scottish when he won the Nobel

Prize for being incredibly clever. They had to track him down to a wee restaurant in Leith – and then wait until he had finished his lunch before they could call him back. *That's* a Scottish hero.

A Burns is infinitely better educated than a Byron.

Thomas Carlyle, *Note Book*

Kirkpatrick Macmillan was born in Courthill Smithy in 1813 . . . Eventually, on one momentous morning in 1839, Kirkpatrick Macmillan beaming proudly, wheeled his pedal bike out of Courthill Smithy, into the sunlight and into history – he has invented the world's first true bicycle, one of the greatest British inventions of the Victorian or any other age. He was fined for speeding at 8mph (13kph).

Christopher Winn,
I Never Knew That About Scotland

As for Gordon Brown – I've described him and Tony Blair as two cheeks of the same arse.

George Galloway

Ten Reasons to be Proud to be Scottish
Adapted from Richard Happer's
365 Reasons to be Proud to be Scottish

David Hume: genius philosopher and all-round brainbox who went to Edinburgh University aged ten. Hume pioneered the essay as a literary genre and started his first major work, *A Treatise of Human Nature*, aged sixteen.

It is now considered one of the greatest philosophical works ever written. He proposed that desire, not reason, governs human behaviour.

Jane Austen, Herman Melville, Johann Goethe, Lord Byron, Sir Arthur Conan Doyle – all owe their big break to a Scottish publisher, **John Murray**. He also published Darwin's *Origin of the Species*.

Thomas Carlyle: exceptional essayist, philosopher and novelist, and possibly the world's most patient man. When he had completed his epic *History of the French Revolution*, he sent it to his mentor John Stuart Mill, whose parlour maid thought it was waste and burned it on the fire. Carlyle rewrote the whole work again.

Many of Thomas Edison's most important breakthroughs were actually made by Scotsman **William Dickson**, who worked for his company. Dickson not only built an early motion-picture camera, he also perfected the standard 35mm film, which he patented on 7 January 1894.

Andrew Carnegie: Dunfermline's weaver's son turned Pittsburgh steel magnate and philanthropist, dubbed 'the richest man in the world' by the 1890s and one of the most famous Scots alive.

When rumours reached the Air Ministry that Nazi Germany had a 'death ray' capable of flattening cities using radio waves, they asked Scottish scientist **Robert Watson-Watt** to investigate. He concluded that the 'death ray' was science fiction, but the idea of using radio waves to locate enemy aircraft could be turned into science fact. Within a few weeks he had created a working model of the world's first radar system (patented in April 1935), a device that would help the Allies win the Second World War.

Alexander Bain: inventor of the first electric clock in 1841 and certainly a man far ahead of his time. He proposed an 'earth battery', built from zinc and copper plates buried in the ground, and, incredibly, invented an experimental fax machine way back in 1843.

The world watched in wonder on 4 July 2012 as scientists announced they had found the most sought-after thing in the world – no, not a taxi at Queen Street station – the Higgs boson. This miraculous morsel of matter creates an invisible energy field that gives everything, from planets to portions of chips, their mass. Its existence was first proposed by **Peter Higgs**, a physicist at Edinburgh University, in 1964. He was in the room 48 years later when experiments caught up with his thinking and proved him right.

Alexander Fleming: couldn't be bothered tidying up his lab when he went on holiday and when he returned on 3 September 1928 there were contaminated bacteria cultures all over his workbench. But Fleming was amazed to see that a fungus had killed patches of bacteria on the clarty dishes. He developed that fungus into penicillin, the single greatest life-saving drug the world has seen. It would conquer syphilis, gangrene, tuberculosis and many other infections.

Dr James Young Simpson: enjoyed nothing more than having a few friends round and after dinner getting them to inhale various chemicals to determine their medical properties. One night he and his chums tried a new concoction and next thing they knew the sun was streaming in through the window. Simpson had just discovered the anaesthetic effect of chloroform (in 1847). The medical establishment was sceptical, but he perfected the anaesthetic and when Queen Victoria used it during labour in 1853, a new era of pain-free surgery began.

6

1966 – Something Happened? Sport

The football field is today's Thunderdome for the Anglo–Scottish rivalry. History's very first international football game was Scotland v England, in 1872. The momentous event was played in Glasgow, and 4,000 fans turned out to see a nil–nil draw.

Our rivalry both on and off the pitch is an eerie mirror of our histories, where Scotland would sometimes seem to get the dud card in the deck. It's the Mary, Queen of Scots model of history. It goes like this: in 2000, England's grip on the world of soccer began to slip. All the usual suspects at the time had been the manager, so The Men In Blazers did the unthinkable and approached a foreigner to stand in the England dugout. His name was Sven-Göran Eriksson. He was Swedish. The England football squad started to sweep all before it. Sven even found the time to sweep up the glamorous TV presenter Ulrika Jonsson.

Scotland took note. We hunted for a foreigner ourselves. We found a German by the name of Berti Vogts. In no time at all we were losing games more spectacularly than ever, and, despite a concerted campaign by Scottish women, Berti failed to have an affair with anyone.

Two tradition-busting foreign managers, two quite different outcomes . . . In the same way, both nations once had queens on their thrones. England had the mighty

Elizabeth I, a remarkable ruler by any standards. We got Mary, Queen of Scots, a woman who got famous for losing her head.

Now, that fall from grace back in 2000 was remarkable at the time, since in 1966 England won something. We've never been allowed to forget it. We just don't mention it.

We've been to the World Cup, of course. Argentina, 1978. Tragically, our national squad laboured under three terrible burdens. In the first place we had a manager who bore an uncanny resemblance to the US president of the time, Jimmy Carter. Ally MacLeod was by all accounts a terribly nice man, but he had the same success on foreign soil as Mr Carter. Secondly, we had a dreadful World Cup song, 'Ally's Tartan Army'. The lyrics, set to the tune of the American Civil War song 'Tramp, Tramp, Tramp, The Boys Are Marching' (at least we were recycling something . . .) contained the deathless lines 'And we'll really shake them up/When we win the World Cup.' The world, it turned out, remained unshaken and barely stirred. And finally, the entire team of '78 had been inexplicably contaminated with perm lotion before they went. Seldom has a football squad taken to the field so awash with curls.

The first two games were a disaster. Peru and Iran unexpectedly turned into footballing giants, but to be honest, we could have been running out against Narnia, the way these blokes were playing. Smashed and defeated, we lined up for the next game, which was the last, tiny shred of hope. Our over-coiffured boys, now virtually leaderless since Ally started skulking in the dugout like a shellshocked WW1 subaltern, lined up against –

Holland, the team widely tipped to lift the trophy (they didn't in the end, but did reach the final, going down to Argentina).

As a nation, Scotland held its breath. And as we so often do, we went down in a blaze of glory. That match has gone into history as one of the greatest World Cup games, and one goal has gone into legend. Archie Gemmill danced around and pirouetted past Dutch defenders to boot the ball into the net. We nearly made it, but the Dutch hit back with another goal. It was Scotland 3, Holland 2. Aye, but as we said to ourselves, Holland went to the final, so that's no' too bad – and we won.

The Tartan Army followed, as the Tartan Army always does. The travelling hordes of Scottish football fans are famous throughout the world for their friendliness and good-natured banter. This is because they very rarely get to stay anywhere long enough to cause any trouble.

In defeat, they are stoic. In victory, they are often baffled. We beat the French in 2007 in Paris. At the final whistle, there had seldom been a larger crowd of flummoxed folk. The Army knows what to do in the face of a 6–nil thrashing. Sing songs insulting Jimmy Hill, drink whatever it is the locals drink, and try to get off with the local lasses – there is a theory, incidentally, that the young men of Scotland's travelling support are assiduous in their attempts to seduce the beauties of Brazil, Argentina and Spain in a desperate effort to create a better chance for a future Scottish team. If your dad is Scots, Fernando, you can pull on that blue jersey.

Of course, what few people have realised is that we have sneakily had English football conquered all along.

Long before English football fell for men from foreign shores given to claims of being special, craggy-jawed, flinty-eyed, laconic Scotsmen ran the game. Bill Shankly, Matt Busby and Alex Ferguson ran the great northern football empires of Liverpool and Manchester, and it was Shankly who summed up the beautiful game with the words 'Football is not a matter of life and death. It's much more important than that.'

And all the time, while the English were watching the footie, we started to get better at other sports. We took up tennis. We had everything we needed in Andy Murray. Flinty-eyed? Check. Craggy-jawed? Check. Then we took up cycling and Lycra, and Chris Hoy lifted gold medal after gold medal. Curling – essentially, it's cleaners on ice, but once again we swept our way to victory. Literally. And let's not forget elephant polo – World Cup Winners, 2004.

And finally, when the world moves into the virtual world to play its games, it plays by our design. Scotland punches way above its weight in the world of computer games – where, in some virtual universe, the Tartan Army constantly celebrates World Cup victories . . .

Edinburgh's Murrayfield Stadium became the home of Scottish rubgy in 1925, when Scotland beat England 14–11.

As a small boy I was torn between two ambitions: to be a footballer or to run away and join a circus. At Partick Thistle I got to do both.

Alan Hansen

'JJ, you live in Kelso, right?' southern tourists would ask him.

'That's right, boys. And a day out of Kelso is a day wasted.'

'You're on England's doorstep?'

'I am.'

'So if you hate England so much how come you live so close to the border?'

'Because it takes a strong man to defend the border.'

John Jeffrey, Scottish international rugby union flanker, quoted in Tom English's *The Grudge*. JJ's day job was his farm in Kelso, about which he had only one regret: 'If I stand on a hill I can see England.'

A philosophical Scotland supporter on a train south to attend the England/Scotland game was heard to comment, 'No matter if we win or lose this game, we will still be winners in the game of life because, when our opponents waken up tomorrow, they'll still be English and we won't.'

Ian Black, *Scotland vs England*

What goes putt-putt-putt-putt?
An English golfer at St. Andrews.

Anonymous

If you thought football kicked off in nineteenth-century England, think again. The game was actually popular in Scotland's medieval courts. In 1497 King James IV paid two shillings for a bag of 'fut ballis', and a leather-bound pig's bladder found in Stirling Castle has been dated to 1540. It is officially the world's oldest football and was discovered lodged in the rafters where presumably some overexcited marquess punted it.

Richard Happer,
365 Reasons to be Proud to be Scottish

Scotland has the only football team in the world that does a lap of disgrace.

Billy Connolly

When the Scotland football team became the first to beat England after their World Cup victory in 1966, their jubilation was extreme . . . There was the wild frolicking in the West End at night, and the great Lion Rampant flags being paraded perilously in the swirl of the traffic in Piccadilly Circus. The taxi driver said: 'They should play in Scotland every year. They're mad.'

John Rafferty, Sports journalist

Pockets of Celtic supporters are holding out on unlikely corners, noisily defending their own carnival atmosphere against the returning tide of normality, determined to preserve the moment, to make the party go on and on. They emerge with a sudden burst of Glasgow accents from taxis or cafés, or let their voices carry with an irresistible aggregate of decibels across hotel lounges . . . At the airport, the impression is of a Dunkirk with happiness. The discomforts of mass evacuation are tolerable when your team have just won the greatest victory yet achieved by a British football club, and completed a clean sweep of the trophies available to them that has never been equalled anywhere in the world.

Hugh McIlvanney reporting Celtic's 2–1 victory of Inter Milan in the final of the European Cup, 25 May 1967. They were the first British team to win this coveted trophy.

It is decreed and ordained that wapinschawings be held by the lords and barons, spiritual and temporal, four times in the year, and that football and golf be utterly cried down and disused, and that bowmarks be made at each parish kirk, a pair of butts, and shooting be made each Sunday. And that each man shoot six shots at the least under the pain to be raised upon them that come not; at the least 2d. to be given to them that come to the bowmark to drink. And this to be used from Christmas to Allhallowmass after . . . And as touching the football and the golf we ordain it to be punished by the baron's fine.

Acts of Parliament, 1447 (James II was fearful that the art of archery was being neglected for the craze for golf and football), Wapinschawings [muster of men under arms]

While, as I have said, Scots are charmed and exhilarated by those who can really play the game, we find it hard – and sometimes impossible – to give England credit for anything. There is no doubt in our collective minds Raich Carter and Bobby Charlton, for instance, ought to have been born Scottish, and we regard it as a cruel accident that they were not. Furthermore, we know they would have been happier men, if they had been. We do not think England deserves players who play like Scotsmen should. By the same token, an English defeat by Scotland is interpreted as a sign from on high that the world is revolving well on its axis. An English win is rationalised as an inconvenience, a temporary interruption of a natural process and, as such, is speedily forgotten.

Now I realise that these assertions will not go down well with any Englishman . . . but who in England wanted to know about them?

John Fairgrieve, *Away Wi' the Goalie!* (1977)

Scotland came out in measured single file, ominously self-possessed, an invisible Piper Laidlaw VC at their head. Whoever dreamed up the theory of body language was vindicated. The tension was numbing and not a ball had been kicked yet. Readers not privileged to be present may think it absurd to write thus of a mere football match. But this was not a mere football match. I am nonplussed to define exactly what it was but it certainly embraced ancient history, modern politics and the constant personas of Anglos and Celts.

Ian Wooldridge, *Daily Mail,* describing the Scottish rugby team's famous 'slow walk' out of the tunnel at Murrayfield to confront England in the 1990 Calcutta Cup final, which Scotland won 13–7.

It is hard to exaggerate the exquisite, unforgettable pleasure the Scots took from leaving the ancient enemy dazed among the rubble of their delusions. A couple of the English players clutched their brows at the end of the match as the shock and lasting pain of what had happened to them began to penetrate. Plenty of Scots will be holding their heads up this morning but the causes will be more temporary and less regrettable.

Hugh McIlvanney, *Observer*, on Scotland's 1990 victory over England in the Calcutta Cup Final.

7
The Land of Four Seasons (in One Day): Weather

Scotland is possibly the only country in the world to have a weather system with Attention Deficit Disorder. It's like living with a three-year-old having endless pick-and-mix sugar-rush tantrums; we never know what it's going to fling at our heads next. Our weather can veer from gentle breeze to Hurricane Bawbag* in the space of about fifteen minutes. It's a source of pride to us that other people are baffled by this.

The minute the sun appears it is seriously game on for pallid Scots sunseekers. The vitamin D vampires know that the clock is running. Time is of the essence. Clothes are abandoned. Skin is exposed. Scottish mothers will scream at their children to get outside *now*, like scrambling Spitfires during the Battle of Britain. But we are careful – as befits a nation that's almost entirely part-ginger and carries the red-haired gene – and so the sunscreen is disinterred from its slumbers. The bottle probably bears a Spanish name and a fading price tag in

---

* **Hurricane Bawbag:** *the first 'Red' warning issued by the Met Office for Central Scotland, 7/8 December 2011, when winds in excess of 90 mph were recorded. It was dubbed 'Bawbag' (Scots: scrotum, annoying person). The term gained international fame when it was used live on air by Robb Gibson, MSP, Convener of the Scottish Parliamentary Environment Committee.*

euros, as it should, having been purchased in a pharmacy in Playa de las Americas during a family holiday three years ago. Since its importation from sunnier climes, the bottle has lived at the back of the bathroom cabinet. In the intervening years, it has both passed its expiry date and separated. This is as nothing to the caring Scottish mother, since the sell-by date is in Spanish and doesn't hold on Scotland's shores and the mixture can be vigorously shaken to reconstitute to an approximation of the original and, as a bonus, stinks enough to deter the midge.

It is impossible to discuss Scottish sunshine without reference to the midge. The midge, or the midgie, as it is better known, is a sort of weather system crossed with the insect world. There is no such thing as a single midgie. The Highland midgie (*Culicoides impunctatus*) is the smallest fly in the UK. Midgies move in mass cloud formations. They bite. They have all the skills of a superb hunter-killer and can detect a single drop of sweat from a perspiring Glaswegian at a range of approximately ten miles. They move like a flying great white shark, and have the ability to envelop a victim in seconds. Traditional defence strategies against insect attack have no effect upon the fearsome midgie. Sprays are ignored, flailing arms merely expose further potential feeding zones and rolled up copies of the *Daily Record* scythe through the cloud like a Jedi light sabre through cigarette smoke. Suggested cures involve befriending a pipe smoker, purchasing a skin cream manufactured by Avon and holidaying abroad. Wearing tights over all exposed areas is also considered a possibility, but this solution is best avoided if hill-walking in the Cairngorms. Not only will you look like a bank robber with a really rubbish sense of direction, but Highlanders will mock you in Gaelic for centuries.

Midge or no, when the sun comes out, every single patch of green space in Scotland will be covered by pale blue Scottish people sizzling to a violent shade of red. It looks like a giant barbecue for Hannibal Lecter.

Rain, of course, is Scotland's dominant weather. It's either raining, or about to rain, or has just been raining. On the upside, we enjoy asking our southern cousins what a hosepipe ban is. On the downside, we have trench foot.

As befits a nation whose summer is really just a rolling cloud variation giving us few blue skies, but fifty shades of grey, we have a rich rain-based vocabulary. Scottish rain can be 'dreich' – that's the sort of rain that flattens your umbrella around your head – or it can be a 'smirr', a fine old word to describe a sort of cross between rain and mist; it may not look horribly wet outside, but smirr seeps into every little nook and cranny to dribble down your neck and the back of your knees. 'Drookit' is an explanation of how you'll be if you venture out into this persistent downfall, and 'pishin it doon sideways' usually means it's that Scottish seaside favourite, heavy rain and high winds. 'Stoatin' rain is a particular menace to the shorter Scot. Each drop of this rain hits the ground at high velocity and bounces back up, giving it the advantage over conventional rain of being able to get up rainwear from underneath. This two-pronged attack leads to wet underwear, and not in a good way.

Historically, this constant battle with the elements gave us a good head start when it came to roving the globe. For one thing, the minute we discovered that other parts of the world had sunshine on a regular basis, we were off. It didn't always go well for us (see the Darien Scheme, chapter 2) but once we got the hang of it, there was no stopping us. A quick glance at the maps of Jamaica, Bermuda, Australia and New Zealand show place names such as Perth, Dundee, Inverness and Hamilton, all places where Scots rocked up and made a home from home. In the case of the West Indies, they acquired the nickname 'Red legs', a reference to the traditional Scottish reaction to exposure to sunshine. When the skin burns to that exquisite scarlet alongside the usual brilliant blue of a Scottish congested vein, it forms a naturally occurring tartan.

Our experience with bad weather meant that it was no holds barred for the Scots in the bleak inhospitable corners of the world. We'd just left them. Turns out, there is someplace like home.

In Scotland, there is no such thing as bad weather – only the wrong clothes.

Billy Connolly

The Scots are steadfast – not their clime.

Thomas Crawford

Scottish weather is perfect for a romantic break. You won't go out much.

London agency's advertisement (2001)

In the north, on a showery day, you can see the rain,

its lovely behaviour over an island – while you stand a mile off in a patch of sun.

George Mackay Brown (1921–96),
An Orkney Tapestry

There are two seasons in Scotland: June and winter.

Billy Connolly

During an excursion to the Isle of Lewis, the weather turned cold and rainy and the passengers huddled together for warmth. The boat captain shouted down to the crew's quarters. 'Is there a mackintosh down there large enough to keep three English ladies warm?'

'No,' came the booming answer, 'but there's a MacPherson who'd like to try!'

Ian Black, *Scotland vs England*

8
Haud Yer Wheesht! Language

It's called 'English', but our southern cousins don't seem to be very good at it. They keep dropping 'h's, and they have trouble with the letter R. They either can't pronounce it – and then insist on naming their sons Roderick, Rodney or Rodger – or they slam it into words where it has no business: 'drawing', which becomes 'drawring', or 'sawing' into 'sawring'. We suspect it's a sneaky Sassenach move to get more triple point scores in Scrabble.

Now, we Scots can handle a consonant. We allow that letter R to breathe. When our television detectives trip over the slumped remains of the professor in the library, not for us the bloodless call for forensics, tissue samples and time of death: no, we pronounce 'Therrrrrre's been a murrrrrrrderrrrrrrrrr'.

Watching the English speak, especially the posh ones, is something of a spectator sport for us. The facial contortions involved in the Received Pronunciation beloved of royals, people who want to be royal and royally snotty BBC newsreaders are an endless source of fascination, especially when they collide with the particularly chewy monikers of foreign heads of state. Every vowel and consonant of names such as Samoa's Prime Minister Tuilaepa Aiono Sailele Malielegaoi, or Bhutan's King Jigme Khesar Namgyel Wangchuck, must be enunciated with such exaggerated care that one *Six*

O' Clock News reader used to look like she was gurning for Essex.

The same rule, incidentally, does not apply to Scottish place names such as Machrihanish, Auchtermuchty or Aonach Beag, all of which can be pronounced as 'What was the funny name of that place we stopped at, darling?'

Scotland's history and geography have given us not just these words but also our accents, matched with a powerful delivery. Scottish fishwives in centuries past were said to communicate to their men in the herring boats and their sister workers across great distances by using a sing-song tone that could skip over the waves. From this we can not only deduce that the fishwives of Scotland had the lung capacity of charging rhinos, but also explain two modern phenomena: the modern predilection for karaoke amongst Scottish working-class women, and the fearsome ability of Scottish mothers to chastise, control and upbraid their children at great distances, sometimes across as many as four or five aisles in Asda.

Given Scotland's vast empty spaces and, later, the noise of the industrial bustle of the great cities, it's not surprising that many Scotsmen still speak at a volume apparently calibrated to address a room full of deaf football referees, fifteen miles away.

By contrast, the English have perfected the indoor voice of quiet calm, with a certain sinister edge. Englishmen of a certain type have long been Hollywood shorthand for the baddie. The great Boris Karloff, the template for the quietly spoken villain, was born in East Dulwich. He became the first actor ever to be billed by his surname only. Just as well he changed it from the family name, which was

Pratt. Screenwriters love that English hissing sound. Well, of course Englishmen are the baddies. What else are we to make of a nation that loots the lexicon of other nations to appropriate words like bungalow, shampoo and tycoon?

By comparison we, the Scots, have become the go-to nation for Caucasian non-American good guys, and this is due in no small part to the language, the accent and the attitude you expect from a nation that can roll its 'R's. Who among us can forget the Scottish actor Gerard Butler (and his chest) as Spartan King Leonidas in the film *300*, booting a Persian messenger to his death with the battle cry of 'This Is SPARTA!!!'? Now, imagine the same scene with Hugh Grant. We rest our case.

Scots is not just one language. We're not so limited in our ambition. We are many languages. In Glasgow, language is evolving unbelievably fast. Actually, it's just unbelievably fast. The rolling tides of migration have brought Highland words and Irish rhythm to the speech of Scotland's biggest city, but the greatest impact on Glaswegian speech is the life expectancy. Glaswegians die faster than Kennedys and, as a result, they have little time for the niceties of vowels and sentence construction, regarding them as the luxury of the pampered south. The plays of Harold Pinter exasperate Glaswegians. Life's too short for pauses.

Further north, around Aberdeen, we have the Doric, a tongue so impenetrable that not even the rest of Scotland understands it, which, we suspect, is the way Aberdonians like it. You may be greeted with the following phrase: 'Fit like, louns an quines?' This translates as 'Hello there, how you doing, boys and girls?' Just say 'fine'. You won't understand the rest of the conversation.

*

We can't leave Scotland's languages without mention of Gaelic, which has enriched the everyday Scots with words such as brogue, shindig, and, of course, whisky (uisge-beatha, which translates as Water of Life). Many a Scot, after a good shindig, dancing in his new brogues, having consumed copious quantities of uisge-beatha, believes they can actually speak Gaelic. They can't, but it does convince passing American tourists that it's Gaelic, which pleases them no end.

There is no 'bad language' in Scots. We are not easily offended by swear words. We leave that to the effete traditions of people who like to write to the BBC in green crayon about newsreaders mispronouncing 'guerrilla'.

Bad language, or swearing, is energetically embraced by the Scots, and has a proud history. The first laws to try to stop anyone anywhere swearing were passed here in Scotland in 1551, which proves we were doing a lot of it. People could face fines of up to 12p, which was a fuck of a lot of money back then. It took the English fifty years to spot this revenue-raising opportunity, but they lost no time in implementing a matching national swear box when they did.

Swearing is a national pastime in Scotland. The full-throated Scot will not only throw the f-word around like a football manager on the winning side – or the losing side, it doesn't really matter – they will even break words up in order to up the quota of stress-busting sweary words they can fit in. In addition, swearing is not a sign of aggression in Scotland. These two phenomena combine in the ultimate Scottish sign of approval – 'fan-fuckin-tastic'.

The Scotch is as spangled with vowels as a meadow with daisies in the month of May.

> Charles Mackay, *The Poetry and Humour of the Scottish Language*

To cultivate an English accent is already a departure away from what you are.

> Sean Connery

The Scotch are great charmers, and sing through their noses like musical tea-kettles.

> Virginia Woolf, *Letters*

I know at least . . . oh, at least 127 words. And I still prefer 'Fuck'.

> Billy Connolly

SOME SCOTTISH WORDS:
Bawbag: scrotum, annoying person. See e.g. **Hurricane Bawbag**, the first 'Red' warning issued by the Met Office for Central Scotland, 7/8 December 2011, when winds in excess of 90 mph were recorded.
Raw-gabbit: speaking confidently on a subject of which one is ignorant
Maulifuff: a young woman who makes a lot of fuss but accomplishes very little
Bubbly jock: a turkey

9

How to Survive the Highlands: Landscape

It's very like the English to corral all their lumpy land-scape into one wee corner and call it 'The Lake District'. You can imagine them showing visitors around, saying, 'And this is where we keep the hills and dales, isn't it, darling?' We can't do that here. Scotland is dominated by mountains and water. One single loch contains more fresh water than all of the lakes in England and Wales combined: the forbidding, brooding Loch Ness. This beautiful loch contains more than just water, of course. Beneath that dark, peaty surface lurks the world-famous monster. Nessie, as she is known, has proudly played blink-and-you'll-miss-it with tourists since 1934. There are those who question her very existence, but every Scot within earshot of an American will loudly proclaim the truth – Nessie lives! The proof is incontestable. There are acres of footage of water ripples to view, and some-thing like a fin was once photographed by special submarine. Why she even has a Latin name, *Nessiteras rhombopteryx*, given to her by an Englishman with a knighthood, so that clinches the deal. And not forgetting that she's worth about £25 million to the local economy, so you bet Nessie bloody exists.

There have been persistent rumours that a similar crea-ture has been seen in Lake Windermere, but we the Scots loudly scoff at such nonsense. No self-respecting horror of the deep would allow herself to live somewhere where her nickname would be 'Windy'.

Highland roads are a delight for any fan of the roller coaster, with their combination of hairpin bends and switchback rises so steep occupants of even the most sedate family saloon will experience momentary weight-lessness as they clear the summit. The Scots have known about this for a very long time. It's no coincidence that the first man on the moon had a Scottish surname. Of course, there is a drawback. Children in the back seat of the car may be securely anchored, but their lunch isn't. It's a feature of Highland motoring. The airborne projectile vomit will hover, waiting for the precise moment when gravity will re-engage, and engulf either passenger or driver – or both. The trajectory of the child's stomach contents, incidentally, is known as the 'Spew Flue'* and, if it should hit the back of the neck, is referred to as a 'Barf Scarf'*.

Fortunately, the Scottish government has moved to prevent loss of life due to drivers being unable to see because of either the windscreen or the driver's glasses being slathered with sick, known in Scotland as 'Boke Blindness'*, by ensuring that every Highland road is patrolled by a caravan towed by a ten-year-old Volvo crewed by a two-person team, usually man and wife, called Eric and Doris, who live in Bermondsey. They have a combined age of 122, and never move above 33 mph, thus preventing spew flue and barf scarf.

We are rarely far from the sea in Scotland. There are

---

* Nessie isn't the only thing the Scots make up to baffle tourists, you know . . .

over 790 islands around our coastline, which are heavily reliant on the ferry service, which is heavily reliant on public subsidy, which it keeps getting, despite Europe ranting on about it, when they can spare the time from legislating against straight bananas. The ferries are run almost entirely by the company Caledonian MacBrayne, or CalMac for short. The importance of the ferry service is celebrated in this verse, based on Psalm 24, 'Unto the Lord belongs the Earth /And all that it contains / Except the Kyles and Western Isles / For they belong to MacBraynes'. Of course, the Lord is just as dominant in the Western Isles, especially the Free Church of Scotland, which, amongst other doctrinal issues, is fundamentally opposed to anyone doing anything on the Lord's Day, such as getting on a ferry. In 2009 CalMac sailed into stormy waters (sorry) when it sent its first car ferry to Stornoway in the teeth of powerful opposition (if you can call twenty people on the pier with placards threatening hellfire, brimstone and damnation 'powerful'). The ferry landed. The cars disembarked. And nothing happened. The hellfire stayed where it was, and the brimstone was undisturbed. It is safe to assume the Lord doesn't work on Sunday, either.

Not all of Scotland is remote, of course. The great central belt between Edinburgh and Glasgow is gently undulating and fairly boring. This makes it a great bed for the busiest motorway in Scotland, the M8. Like most of Britain's roadways, it was never built for the amount of traffic it carries and so is the subject of regular trench warfare between road repair teams and drivers. Harthill is the only service station to straddle a Scottish motorway and stands across the choked lanes of the M8 midway between Glasgow and Edinburgh. A proud sign states 'Harthill – the heart of Scotland.' See what they did there? And it is the heart of Scotland in so many ways. Particularly in the manner in which both arteries leading into it are permanently narrowed and dangerously blocked.

The great thing about Glasgow is that if there's a nuclear attack it'll look exactly the same afterwards.

Billy Connolly

When he awoke it was dawn. Or something like dawn. The light was watery, dim and incomparably sad. Vast, grey, gloomy hills rose up all around them and in between the hills there was a wide expanse of black bog.

Stephen had never seen a landscape so calculated to reduce the onlooker to utter despair in an instant. 'This is one of your kingdoms, I suppose, sir?' he said.

'My kingdoms?' exclaimed the gentleman in surprise. 'Oh, no! This is Scotland!'

Susanna Clarke, *Jonathan Strange & Mr Norrell*

Land of polluted river,
Bloodshot eyes and sodden liver
Land of my heart forever
Scotland the Brave.

Billy Connolly, quoted in Jonathan Margolis,
The Big Yin (1994)

The urban misery, the architectural degradation, the raw, alcohol-riddled despair, the petty criminal furtiveness, the bleak violence of living in many parts of industrial Scotland.

John McGrath, *Naked Thoughts That Roam About*
(with Nadine Holdsworth, 2001)

Dundee, a frowsy fisherwife addicted to gin and infanticide.

Lewis Grassic Gibbon, *Scottish Scene*

It all looks a bit like somebody's mouth just after they've had most of their teeth removed.

Iain Banks on Gourock, in *Raw Spirit*

Just as we sat down, a gust of wind came and dispersed the mist, which had a most wonderful effect, like a dissolving view – and exhibited the grandest, wildest scenery imaginable. It had a sublime and solemn effect; so wild, so solitary – no one but ourselves and our little party here.'

Queen Victoria, Balmoral, 1859

10
Legally Tender: Love and Romance

Scotland gave the world not one but two towering, glowering icons of romance: Burns and Bond.

In Robert Burns we had the ultimate sweet-talking guy. Burns was born on an Ayrshire farm in 1759. Farming in those days was a backbreaking, muscle-building activity. These days we'd call it an all-body workout. As a result, when he rocked up on a borrowed pony in Edinburgh in 1786, he filled a fashionable suit nicely. The fans of the finest society ladies were positively aflutter when this son of the soil pitched up in their salons looking all dark and broody. Burns was a roaring success. We know that Robert was a hit with the laydeeez because he kept having kids with them. He died at the age of thirty-seven, but he still managed to father twelve children – that we know of. When Scots say we are the sons and daughters of Burns, we really might be.

In Edinburgh, though, he met the girl who didn't succumb to his charms. Agnes Maclehose was a clever blonde with a bit of attitude, not surprising in a Glasgow girl. Educated, sharp and witty, she was the wife of a serious bad boy, James Maclehose. She'd already left him on grounds of cruelty, and he'd already spent time in the debtors' prison. He was now in Jamaica; probably his family arranged that to get him out of the way. Passion between the lady and the poet was the order of the day, but the dirty deed was off limits. Agnes was, of course, Mrs Maclehose, and even though the errant James was off in Kingston – and had started another family with his girlfriend out there – succumbing to the charms of the ploughman poet was out of the question for a married lady. As she herself wrote, 'Your Friendship much can make me blest / O, why that bliss destroy! / Why urge the odious, one request / You know I must deny!'. It doesn't take a genius to work out what Robert had been requesting. They never did get it on. They wrote to each other, and yearned a lot. They must have been shuddering like a pair of overloaded tumble dryers when they met. They had little nicknames for each other – he was 'Sylvander', and she was 'Clarinda'. When they finally parted, Burns wrote 'Ae Fond Kiss', one of the most sublime love poems in any language. Come on. Let's be honest. A bit of slap and tickle is one thing, but to have some of the world's most beautiful verse dedicated to you – now that's romance.

Oh, and while Clarinda was playing hard to get, Sylvander knocked up her maid, Jenny Clow, who gave birth to a son. She called the boy Robert Burns Clow. Kinda gave the game away there . . .

The son of a Scottish father, educated at one of Scotland's most prestigious private schools, Fettes College, he has dedicated his life to fighting the forces of terror. His name is Blair, Tony Blair. Oh no, hang on, wrong one. His name is Bond, James Bond. 007 is Scottish to his core. There are no worthwhile relationships in the life of this relentless workaholic. He spends more time with his Walther PPK than any woman. His life is totally consumed by his job.

In fact, he doesn't seem to be able to give up work at all. Mind you, when all's said and done, 007 is a civil servant, so his pension is probably utterly rubbish, which is why he can't retire. On a day-to-day basis, Bond consumes booze at a rate that would make Oliver Reed look like a New Age Californian yoga instructor, and pumps enough smoke and ash into the atmosphere from his heroic eighty-a-day hand-rolled fag habit to ground flights over London for a week. Despite this, he still looks good in a dinner suit, manages to handle an Aston Martin and has a neat line in snappy one-liners. Women hurl themselves at him like seagulls going for a dropped fish supper. His most iconic embodiment speaks with a faintly frightening oh-so-slurred Edinburgh accent. Somewhere in just about every Scotsman's head there is a little tiny corner where they believe they are Bond, James Bond. Just watch them if they get the chance to try on a tux in a dress hire shop. When they think no one is looking, it's a big twirl in front of the mirror, fingers pointing into the reflection and a snappy 'McGinty. Jimmy McGinty.' (They use their own name to keep it real.)

Are Scotswomen romantic? Of course we are. We care for our men. We know our men have a lot to think about, so we've made sure the most crucial sentence they ever say is just two words, and that's 'I do.' And most importantly, we hardly ever remind our men of how they really looked in their hired dinner suit at the end of the office Burns Night, when they decided to sing 'Ae Fond Kiss' in the front garden and next door's dog got a fright and pissed on their leg.

I have always hated that damn James Bond. I'd like to kill him.

Sean Connery

If you're goin' to speak aboot love, be dacent and speak aboot it in the Gaalic. But we're no talkin' aboot love: we're talkin' aboot my merrage.

Neil Munro, The Vital Spark

Roses are red, violets are blue, I'm schizophrenic, and so am I.

Billy Connolly

Marriage: a friendship recognised by the police.

Robert Louis Stevenson

Continental people have a sex life; the English have hot-water bottles.

George Mikes

If Harry Potter's so magical, why can't he cure his own eyesight and get laid? A teenage lad shouldn't need a broomstick to cling on to.

Frankie Boyle

Quiz: How Scottish Are You?

1. **QUESTION:** Which of the following is NOT a breakfast food – eggs, black pudding, Buckfast Tonic Wine?
ANSWER: Well, it's a trick question. They all are, under the right circumstances.

2. **QUESTION:** Eighteenth-century Edinburgh was a hotbed of alcoholic consumption. A popular drink was white wine and marmalade – true or false?
ANSWER: It's true. The wine would have been warm then, and marmalade was whisked through it. It's horrible. The author drank a shitload of the stuff to try to acquire the taste for it and failed miserably.

3. **QUESTION:** It was once possible to avoid your debtors in Scotland by hiding in the Queen's Scottish home – the palace of Holyroodhouse. True or false?
ANSWER: It's true. The road outside the palace of Holyroodhouse has three huge brass letter 'S's sunk into the road. This marks the line of sanctuary for the palace grounds. If you were in debt and you crossed that line, your creditors couldn't touch you. Not even your AmericanExpressMasterCardVisa. Handy. The English just used to let you claim sanctuary for murder. And the French had a thing about hunchback bellringers. It's money, my friends, though, that's what matters.

4. QUESTION: You are in an English corner shop. You have proffered a Scottish ten-pound note for your magazine, Mars Bar and can of something called Tizer. The shop owner has flatly stated 'I can't take your money.' The correct response?

A: Fury, temper, screaming and a calling of hate and hellfire down on the establishment and its owner

B: A terse history lesson with a sidebar of economic reality thrown in

C: Say 'You won't take my money!? That's very generous of you. Thanks very much.' And walk out.

ANSWER: It's C, of course. I can't take your money in Scotland means just that. I am giving you this – I cannot accept your money. But good luck with that, if you do decide to try it.

5. QUESTION: The kilt. Few sights are more inspiring than that of a big brawny kilted laddie birling about during an eightsome reel. Even more impressive is the view from behind him. Scotsmen love kilts. Why?

A: They like to get the air about their wee bits

B: It's a good excuse to start a fight with anyone who calls it a skirt

C: Sheep can hear zips.

ANSWER: A. And B. Not C.

6. QUESTION: You are in a pub in Glasgow. There is a football match on. It is England v anyone else. The correct public protocol is?

A: Politely cheer on England

B: Loudly cheer on anyone else

C: Do both.

ANSWER: Actually, you can do all of the above. Doesn't really matter – we'll all just wait for the penalty shoot-out at the end. English can't shoot for toffee . . .

9. **QUESTION:** Watching the weather forecast on television, there are predictions of heatwaves in London, while snow is forecast for Scotland. It is June. The correct Scottish response should be?

A: Fury. Somehow the bastard English have controlled the weather and are stealing our sunshine

B: Honking laughter – that'll serve the London bastards right. They'll all get skin cancer. Hell mend them

C: Ah well, crack out the ski suit then.

ANSWER: Pretty much all of them, really. The correct response to the Scottish weather report is anger, denial and, finally, resignation.

10. **QUESTION:** Which is the correct answer to the following question: 'Huzitguan, bigman?'

A: I am well, thank you

B: Nosaebad-howsyersel

C: Pardon me?

ANSWER: B. A and C will immediately brand you as an incomer, and should the question, which can be translated as 'Hello big chap, how are you?' be directed at you post-midnight on Sauchiehall Street, Glasgow on breath tanged with one too many pints, it's more of an invitation to a 'Square Go'. That is, a battering/rammy/daeyerheidin. You don't want to know what the last statement means. The correct tribal response, as detailed above, can be translated as, 'I am very well, how are you?'

11. **QUESTION:** What is 'Scotch Mist'?

A: A strange sudden fog that descends over the landscape

B: A cold sea fog that moves in from the coast

C: The fug of fogginess that clouds up the brain after the fourth single malt.

ANSWER: Dunno – let's get the malt down and give it a go!

Appendix

YouGov survey for *The Sunday Times* investigating Scottish attitudes towards the English: April 2007, 1027 respondents, aged 18+. Respondents were asked the following question:

> 'Thinking of the qualities of English people, which, if any, of the following statements do you tend to agree with? (please tick all that apply)'

English people tend to be more arrogant than Scots	40%
English people tend to be less warm and friendly than Scots	35%
English people tend to be less polite than Scots	27%
English people tend to be more racist/ xenophobic than Scots	25%
English people tend to be more right-wing than Scots	23%
English people tend to be more likely to whinge about things than Scots	17%
None of these apply	28%
Don't know	8%

If you **HATED** this then you'll LOVE...

TURN ME OVER

THISTLE Vs ROSE

Scotland, England, and 700 Years of Love, Hatred and Indifference

Albert Jack

Turn over and find out what the other half think!

Reside in the land of 'long shadows, country cricket grounds and old maids bicycling through the morning mist' ...apparently.

Expert queuers polite to the point of ridicule – they are prone to mumble in perfect unison 'Oh sorry', 'Oh do excuse me' even in the heat of battle.

Speak the language of Shakespeare, Byron and Milton and spout pentameters as easily as breathing.

Portray possibly the oddest, most awkward and yet successful courting ritual of any nation. Traditionally characterised by floppy-haired lotharios boasting bumbling English awkwardness, all teeth, chin and a sense of propriety.

A regular winner on the battlefield of sport against Scotland, football, rugby, you name it (and probably cricket too if Scotland actually played it)!

Ginger beard as bright and beautiful as the cans of Irn Bru his countrymen drink.

The ingenuity of the Scot knows no bounds, boasting amongst many inventions tarmac, the steam engine, tablet, television and of course the breakfast spread of champions - marmalade.

The raw power to be able to lob tree trunks around a field, beat anyone in the world on a bicycle (thank you Sir Chris Hoy) and an unnatural talent for sweeping up on ice (*curling).

Filled to bursting with the best of fare - haggis, whisky and basically anything deep fried.

A Scot can handle a consonant. They allow the letter R to breathe. When their television detectives trip over the slumped remains of a professor in the library, they pronounce 'therrrrre's been a murrrrrderrrrrr.'

CULTURE
ENGLISH
Morris Men = dancing with bells on
LANGUAGES
ENGLISH
The Queen's English
FOOD & DRINK
ENGLISH
The Full English
SPORT
ENGLISH
1966. Enough said
LOVE & SEX
ENGLISH
Lie Back and Think of England
WEATHER
ENGLISH
In Hertford, Hereford and Hampshire Hurricanes Hardly Happen

If you **HATED** this
then you'll LOVE...

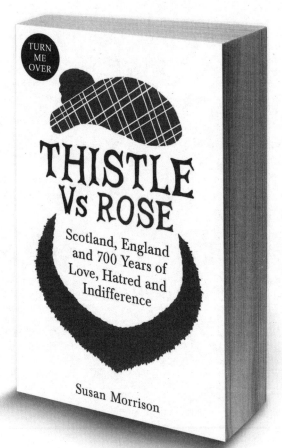

TURN
ME
OVER

THISTLE
Vs ROSE

Scotland, England
and 700 Years of
Love, Hatred and
Indifference

Susan Morrison

Turn over and find out
what the other half think!

Thistle Versus Rose

Scotland, England and 700 Years of Love, Hatred and Indifference

'*It is tremendously good fun winding up the Scots. It is terribly easy, particularly Scottish politicians. They can take things far too seriously.*' *Jeremy Paxman*

It's 700 years since England fought Scotland at the Battle of Bannockburn. Miraculously – we still don't understand how – the Scots actually won. It's pretty much the only time they've ever beaten the English at anything. So has there ever been a better opportunity to celebrate seven centuries of winding up the Scots?

Exploring everything from food, class, the empire and the weather to language, love and landscape, *Thistle vs Rose* is a hilarious miscellany of Anglo-Scots rivalry. Introduced by bestselling popular historian Albert Jack, it features quotes, jokes and trivia from Stephen Fry, Jimmy Carr, Michael McIntyre, Winston Churchill and many, many others.

Albert Jack

Thistle Versus Rose

Scotland, England and 700 Years of Love, Hatred and Indifference

SCEPTRE

First published in Great Britain in 2014 by Sceptre
An imprint of Hodder & Stoughton
An Hachette UK company

First published in paperback in 2014

1

A CIP catalogue record for this title is available from the British Library

ISBN 978 1 473 60501 5

Typeset by Palimpsest Book Production Ltd, Falkirk, Stirlingshire

Printed and bound by Clays Ltd, St Ives plc

Hodder & Stoughton policy is to use papers that are natural, renewable
and recyclable products and made from wood grown in sustainable forests.
The logging and manufacturing processes are expected to conform to the
environmental regulations of the country of origin.

Hodder & Stoughton Ltd
338 Euston Road
London NW1 3BH
www.hodder.co.uk

Contents

Introduction: My England, My Scotland

As a proud Englishman, I am also a Scottish nationalist. That is, of course, in the same way that I may be considered a lesbian. I am in favour of all the same things. I fully understand. I am sympathetic. I see where you are all coming from. The love of a lovely woman and an independent Scotland would both do me nicely, thanks. We are on the same side.

The rivalry between the English and the Scots has been going on as long as history itself. No sooner did man learn to walk upright and light a fire than the people from the colder end of this island started arguing with the Sassenachs over who owned what cave, where the goats could be grazed and whose unevolved woman belonged to whom. (Not unlike parts of Scotland today.)

And this is the perfect time to examine such a rivalry, what with 2014 being the 700th anniversary of Scotland's original bid for independence when spider-inspired Robert the Bruce laid a trap for the effeminate King Edward II near a small stream called Bannockburn, south of Stirling. But what has really got me going is Scotland's referendum in September when everyone north of the border gets to vote on whether they want out of the United Kingdom or not.

*

I have two major issues with this referendum. The first is why so many of the prominent, high-profile Scottish nationalists who have been calling so loudly for independence no longer live in Scotland. I could name the actors and the tartan-wearing pop singers I refer to but what would that achieve? My point is: the notable thing about the Scots is, as soon as they can afford to leave, they usually do. My other irritation is that while these expatriate patriots are respectfully listened to, we English aren't even eligible to vote in this referendum that affects us all. But that is probably just as well because it could result in the strange situation of the Scots voting to stay in and the English voting them out.

So, if the Scots were to hand back everything we'd given them when we waved them on their un-merry way, then how would they be affected? Well for one thing I doubt they'll be very happy when they start having to queue up at Immigration. Imagine that. Applying for an English visa just to pop across the border to Berwick for their weekly shopping. And then having to pay import duty on the way home. And don't anybody north of the border expect the European Union to recognise an independent Scotland any time soon. That would be seen as a green light for every other backward-thinking province and region in Europe to start demanding independence. For example, an independent Scotland would give the Basque people of Spain ideas above their station, and what would happen then? So Scotland's independence from England means independence from Europe as well. Not a glorious separate European state at all. Far from it. Don't think Italy, Portugal or the Netherlands: think Andorra, San Marino or Liechtenstein instead.

We even introduced the Scots to their national dish. Haggis was actually invented in Scandinavia by the Vikings (haggva is Old Norse for 'to chop up'), who brought it along when they invaded England. 'Hegese', as it was then called, was very popular in medieval times (English tastes were more primitive then) and was first written about in 1430: Scotland only formally adopted it during the eighteenth century. So that's haggis off the menu for an independent Scotland. Not to mention the Scotch egg, which was brought back to England from India by the soldiers of the Empire and worked up for Victorian picnics by London's Fortnum & Mason. Or Scotch broth, which turns out to be a very English soup (its name is a dig at the legendary meanness of the Scots as it's something that can be made from very cheap ingredients). And that's just the starters.

Our pathetic Chancellor has threatened them with the removal of the pound but what about if we took back our language too? There is no question that the good people from north of the border would struggle without English. A recent census revealed that as few as one per cent of the population can speak Gaelic.

But this brings us to the question of who is actually Scottish and who is actually English anyway? Those lines blurred a long time ago. I have a friend who insists he is Scottish because he supports Glasgow Rangers. I keep telling him he isn't but he will not listen and wants me to mind my own business. But my evidence is compelling. Namely that he was born in Newcastle and has a Geordie accent. But that is not good enough for him and so he is Scottish. Mind you, he has made a few quid and lives in Los Angeles now so that doesn't matter anyway.

Even Scotland's very own patron saint, St Andrew, wasn't a local boy. He was a disciple of John the Baptist and was born somewhere near the Sea of Galilee. He has also been adopted by Russia, Malta, Cyprus, Ukraine, Sicily and, because he apparently told Jesus that story about the loaves and the fishes, is also the patron saint of the Association of Fishmongers. He was later crucified on a saltire cross (that's an X-shape if you are reading this in Glasgow), which accounts for the Scottish flag, but there is no record of him ever visiting Scotland. He had probably never even heard of it. Mind you, England's St George was himself a Roman soldier, the son of a Greek Christian. While it's just about possible he may have spent time in Albion, as the legends have it, he certainly didn't slay any dragons. So I think honours are about even in the saints debate.

So you can see it is complicated. So complicated that our little group of islands in the North Sea can't even decide what to call ourselves now, while we *are* united. Is it England, as many insist? Or is it the British Isles? How about Great Britain? No? OK, try the United Kingdom then. Could it just be Britain, as the Americans believe? I don't know why I just brought them into the debate; what do they know about our history? They have precious little of their own. In England and Scotland we have schools that are three times as old as America. Even some of the public conveniences in our towns and cities are older than America. Forget I mentioned them.

Of course there has to be a head to my tail: just how would England cope if she were deprived of all her Scottish influences? One thing we do know for sure is that in the past, despite our natural dislike, mistrust and rivalries, whenever our little group of islands has been threatened we have always put our differences aside and fought together against our common enemy. And as soon as that threat subsides we are quick to adopt our old prejudices again.

In contributing to the debate between England and Scotland, I intend to explore both cultures of our once-great countries, where they differ, where they match and where, on occasion, they meet somewhere in the middle. We all live on the same island, only separated by a thin and unguarded border. Could it be possible that we are more alike than is comfortable to admit? The good people of Newcastle and Carlisle might well have more in common with the Scots than they do with the natives of southern England. And what does a line on a map mean anyway?

While the Scots have moaned and bellyached about the English for centuries, we have for the most part maintained a dignified silence. But as I've never been too good at being dignified, or silent, I've decided that it's high time to get to the bottom of the situation. Now, be warned that I come to this debate armed with the sword of fact and a shield decorated with historic events. I may even have God on my side. I've gathered together all kinds of amusing stories from history, surprising statistics and witty quotations from everyone from Samuel Johnson to Frankie Boyle. What I want to find out is how English culture has influenced the Scots and vice versa and what exactly we have done to annoy each other so much over the last thousand years. So now it's time for you to settle back into your favourite armchair with a glass of something neutral – maybe a nice Irish whisky or French wine – and enjoy the argument. Is it really too late to learn from our shared history?

Albert Jack, England

Vital Statistics

The beginning is a good time to remind ourselves of who we actually are, and this is easy to do with the help of the latest United Kingdom Census (2011).

Name: England
Location: Just off the coast of mainland Europe
Official Language: English
Government: A Constitutional Monarchy
Monarch: Queen Elizabeth II (London, England)
Seat of Government: London
Gross Domestic Product: $2.6 trillion
Religion: Not really
Population: 56.1 million
Ethnicity: White (92%) Other (8%)
National Pastime: Cricket
Motto: 'This Green and Pleasant Land'

Name: Scotland
Location: Attached to the north of England and surrounded by the North Sea on three sides
Official Language: English (Until further notice)
Government: A Constitutional Monarchy (For now)
Monarch: Queen Elizabeth I (Well, she is *their* first Elizabeth)

Seat of Government: London (Forward mail to Edinburgh)

Gross Domestic Product: $235 billion (or three shillings and sixpence)

Religion: Christian (Anglican, Church of Scotland, Roman Catholic, Presbyterian, Methodist) with a hint of Judaism, Islam, Buddhism, Hinduism and others

Population: 5.2 million (and falling)

Ethnicity: White & Ginger (98.2%) Other (1.8%)

National Pastime: Drinking

Motto: 'In My Defence God Defend Me.' (I don't know what that means either)

I
Manners And Etiquette

There is nothing that we English value more than our manners. We are passionate about politeness. Our complex systems of secret codes baffle foreigners. 'With all due respect,' we say, indicating that an insult will follow. 'Does anyone want the last biscuit?' we ask, and in doing so claim it for ourselves. Our speech is littered with how are you, please and thank you, although these are bloodless reflexes rather than demonstrations of actual gratitude; we don't *really* care how you are. Sometimes, observes the American comedian Reginald D. Hunter, an English person's insult – wrapped in irony, disguised by good manners – takes him three weeks to figure out. When two English people bump into each other they are locked in an eternal sidestepping dance, shuffling in perfect unison while mumbling 'Oh sorry', 'Oh do excuse me'; it's the closest we get to talking to strangers.

There are also rules that govern modesty. We worship the God of Self Deprecation. We must not appear to show off, even when we actually *are* showing off. Our Nobel Prize or Oscar can only be referred to indirectly or with a healthy dose of irony – 'Well they had to give me that, if only to stop me hanging around' – and then placed in the downstairs toilet where visitors can admire our achievements and, simultaneously, our reluctance to gloat about them.

The Scots, on the other hand, are rather more direct. In England the words 'Excuse me' are usually used as a way to attract a person's attention or as a response to being barged into (so polite are we that we automatically thank the traffic warden as he hands us a ticket). In Scotland if you hear somebody say 'Excuse me,' followed by 'Jimmy', it normally signals the start of a confrontation. There are also certain taboos running throughout Scottish society, the most important of which appear to be never turning down a drink if offered, always buying a round in return and, most importantly of all, never ever calling a Scottish person English. Or Scotch.

I read a guidebook that warns tourists to avoid football fans, recommends Irn-Bru, encourages pub crawls and urges readers to become 'merrily drunk' on whisky, carry an umbrella at all times and avoid council estates. The guidebook goes on to say 'Please do not expect to receive the same quick, polite and accurate service here as in Japan. Be patient anywhere in Scotland: this is not Japan.' Wise advice indeed, apart from the Irn-Bru part. Finally it explains that the Scots are a 'low contact' type of people and that, instead of touching or standing close, it is better to remain at least one arm's length from a Scotsman. This is also good advice although, if you are English, you may want to make this at least a couple of miles.

An Englishman, even if he is alone, forms an orderly queue of one.

George Mikes

When I first read this comment I thought it was an amusing exaggeration, but then I found that not only was it true, but I also do it myself. When waiting alone for a bus or at a taxi stop, I do not lounge about anywhere roughly within striking distance of the stop as people do in other countries – I stand directly under the sign, facing in the correct direction, exactly as if I were at the head of a queue. I form a queue of one. If you are English, you probably do this too.

Kate Fox, *Watching the English*

Once upon a time the English knew who they were . . . They were polite, excitable, reserved and had hot-water bottles instead of a sex life: how they reproduced was one of the mysteries of the western world . . . They were class-bound, hidebound and incapable of expressing their emotions. They did their duty. Fortitude bordering on the incomprehensible was a byword: 'I have lost my leg, by God!' exclaimed Lord Uxbridge, as shells exploded all over the battlefield. 'By God, and have you!' replied the Duke of Wellington.

Jeremy Paxman, *The English*

In England, we have such good manners that if someone says something impolite, the police will get involved.

Russell Brand

If an Englishman gets run down by a truck, he apologises to the truck.

Jackie Mason

The gentleness of the English civilisation is perhaps its most marked characteristic. You notice it the moment you set foot on English soil. It is a land where conductors are good-tempered and policemen carry no revolvers. In no country inhabited by white men is it easier to shove people off the pavement.

George Orwell

The Englishman has all the qualities of a poker except its occasional warmth.

Daniel O'Connell

In left-wing circles it is always felt that there is something slightly disgraceful in being an Englishman, and that it is a duty to snigger at every English institution, from horse racing to suet puddings. It is a strange fact, but it is unquestionably true, that almost any English intellectual would feel more ashamed of standing to attention during 'God Save the King' than stealing from a poor box.

George Orwell

2

The Class System

Over sixty years have passed since George Orwell described England as 'the most class-ridden country under the sun' and I'm sure he would be as disappointed as I am that the class system is still alive and well, both north and south of Hadrian's Wall. For centuries, whether working-class, middle-class, down-and-out, up-and-coming, a toff or an obscenely rich banker who could do with my big sister's sort of backhander (the kind that isn't delivered in envelopes), the English and the Scots have grown up understanding where they fit into society. It's all about Them and Us and making sure that anyone beyond the pale (which is, incidentally, a charming phrase that the English ruling classes in Ireland used to describe anyone who didn't live in or near to Dublin – anyone from beyond the Pale Hills was a 'bogtrotter') knew their place.

Our aristocracy is made up of people who have forgotten the humiliating lengths to which their distant ancestors went to achieve power and position. I was once unfortunate enough to find myself in the Royal Enclosure at Epsom on Derby Day, in an attempt to study the upper classes in their preferred habitat, only to hear one very well spoken lady say to another, 'Well, of course, we all know the royal family are naff.' Maybe so, madam, but can we assume you live on your sprawling country estate because one of your ancestors wiped a royal bottom every day for twenty years? Or had sex with it?

Because that is how the class system of England developed in the first place. Peerages and other noble honours have been handed out in England to royal favourites since King Edward III initiated the first English dukedoms by naming his eldest son, Edward the Black Prince, the Duke of Cornwall in 1337. Ever since then the reigning monarch of England has been creating viscounts, earls, marquesses and barons out of his or her favourite lackey, loafer or lover. When our countries supposedly became one in 1707, the English made damn sure that the Scots nobility knew their place: all but sixteen of their peers were not permitted to attend the House of Lords until 1963. For the intervening 250 years they were simply left out of the political process in London completely. It turned out to be not so much an Act of Union but an Act of Suppression. I just wish we'd suppressed *all* the upper classes, across the board and across all the borders.

The peculiar thing historically has been how both the upper class and the working class have been proud of how they are while those in the middle have aspired, or pretended, to be one or the other. Happily, even they have come a long way from the world Nancy Mitford wrote about in *Noblesse Oblige* (1956) where she separated the way the upper (U) and middle (Non-U) classes spoke. The middle class in 1950s Britain, recently emerged from post-war austerity, were very anxious about where they fitted into society and wanted to be posh. With the cut-glass arrogance of her aristocratic background, Mitford saw it as an enormous joke, but those she saw as her social inferiors took it very seriously indeed. In Monty Python's *Meaning of Life*, when the grim reaper turns up at a middle-class dinner party, his hosts are far more embarrassed about the Social Death of being exposed as serving tinned salmon than about the fact that they've just poisoned all their guests and themselves.

Nancy Mitford's book reminded them that every time they opened their mouths, they gave themselves away. And we all still do to this day. Do you say sofa or settee, scent or perfume, graveyard or cemetery? Do you call your midday meal lunch or dinner? Perhaps you make a point of having afternoon tea instead of the can of lager they prefer in Caledonia (Christ, maybe I'm part Scot!). And then there is the last meal of the day. For some people that is called dinner, while others are asked what they want for their tea. If you say 'How do you do?' then I have a polite reply. But if you say 'All right mate?' then you can expect a different one. Is it what or pardon, balderdash or bullshit, cor blimey or jeepers? Am I a gentleman or a geezer, a bounder or a bad boy? As soon as I hear which word you use, I know who you are, where you come from and how to reply.

But now the wheel has turned full circle and reverse snobbery has young Tarquins and Arabellas trying desperately to sound working-class and 'street' but betraying themselves as soon as they ask where the 'bog' is. Our Prime Minister and most of his cabinet were educated at Windsor Comprehensive aka Eton. And the English people have finally had enough. The posh are (sadly) always with us, but now even they can see what thin ice they're on. It's such a pity that the Scots, who love a good fight, are thinking of leaving just before the election that could give our toffs their marching orders at last. When the Chancellor, the Oxford-educated millionaire Conservative MP George Osborne, admitted he 'didn't know' when he last bought a pasty, he was compared to Marie Antoinette for being 'out of touch' with the general public. 'Vive la révolution' is what I say.

The English country gentleman galloping after a fox – the unspeakable in full pursuit of the uneatable.

> Lord Illingworth in *A Woman of No Importance*
> by Oscar Wilde

The whole strength of England lies in the fact that the enormous majority of the English people are snobs.

> George Bernard Shaw

When it's three o'clock in New York, it's still 1938 in London.

> Bette Midler

An aristocracy in a republic is like a chicken whose head has been cut off: it may run about in a lively way, but in fact it is dead.

> Nancy Mitford, *Noblesse Oblige*

Nosism (1829) – the use of the royal 'we' in speaking of oneself

> Adam Jacot de Boinod, *I Never Knew There Was*
> *a Word For It*

Q: How long has your family lived at the present address?
A: 697 years.

Sir Thomas Ingilby, of Ripley Castle

I was once naïve enough to ask the late Duke of Devonshire why he liked the town of Eastbourne. He replied with a self-deprecating shrug that one of the things he liked was that he owned it.

A. N. Wilson

One has often wondered whether, upon the whole earth, there is anything so unintelligent, so unapt to perceive how the world is really going, as an ordinary young Englishman of our upper class.

Matthew Arnold

Those comfortably padded lunatic asylums which are known, euphemistically, as the stately homes of England.

Virginia Woolf

Dennis: Come and see the violence inherent in the system. Help! Help! I'm being repressed!
King Arthur: Bloody peasant!
Dennis: Oh, what a giveaway! Did you hear that? Did you hear that, eh? That's what I'm on about! Did you see him repressing me? You saw him, didn't you?

Monty Python and the Holy Grail

The English are like their own beer; froth on top, dregs at bottom, the middle excellent.

Voltaire

If someone is very upper-class, you have a stereotype of him which is probably true. If someone has a working-class accent, you have no idea who you're talking to.

Michael Caine

3
Divided by a Common Language

English is technically the official language of both Scotland and England but the Scots have twisted the language they speak over the last few centuries into something almost unintelligible. Whether they have been trying to evolve an entirely new language to safely discuss their independence plans in front of oblivious English people, or simply to stop any non-Scot enjoying golfing holidays, we will probably never know.

In England, however, we developed a manner of communicating – called speaking – a very long time ago, during a period when the Scots were at the gesticulating-and-grunting stage. Out of the wheezes and squawks of Geordie, Brummie, Scouse, Manc and Mackem, our public-schooled elite nurtured a rarefied form of their mother tongue, nourished by Milton and Wordsworth, and enunciated in tones purged of the guttural Northern vowels and Essex glottal stops: Received Pronunciation. How – the argument ran – could provincials so benighted as to mouth words like clarty, stottie, minging or alreet be thought to animate such linguistic monstrosities with wit or intellect? It stood to reason that the upper classes – to whom girls were 'gels' and your father was 'deddih' – had happened upon a language fit for angels. 'Do pa-ass your mathar the ba-ath bans and the batter-dish'.

Throughout England different regions have slowly developed their own dialects, perhaps the most famous being Cockney rhyming slang. When I was growing up this was used widely in our house, so I always knew when it was time to head for the 'apples' or 'up the wooden hill to Bedfordshire', or if Granddad was 'having a sherbet in the rub a dub' of a Sunday dinnertime.

So what can anybody who speaks proper English expect when they visit our Caledonian cousins? I'll start by asking the one question any visitor to Scotland needs: 'Please could you direct me to the nearest bar?' (Fortunately because of the BBC they can easily understand our English accents, but of course this might not last in an independent Scotland.) So far so good, until they reply, 'Alreet big mon, yer lukkin fur a' wee dram? Neigh dangur, hees wat ya wann doi, reet. Reet dunn tha reed reet, bat ha bus stop on yer lift. Un maind ha ya gee,' which translates as: 'Hello, sir, are you looking for a drink? No problem. What you want to do is go straight down the road and the bar is on the left by the bus stop.' No wonder all the guidebooks on Scotland advise you that the best thing to do is to get so drunk that it all makes sense (not their actual words, but you get the drift).

It's not really their fault though. The English have Shakespeare: the Immortal Bard, spouting pentameters as easily as breathing, his pen charged with manna rather than ink. The Scots equivalent is Robert Burns (aka Rabbie Bins); and what hope can you have when the finest flower of your literature is a pedlar of folksy jingles, barely legible behind the mush of phonetic spelling? This is the first verse of his famous 'Address to a Haggis', the centre-piece of any Burns Night celebration:

> Fair fa' yer honest, sonsie face,
> Great chieftain o' the pudding race!
> Aboon them a' ye tak yer place,
> Painch, tripe, or thairm:
> Weel are ye wordy o' a grace
> As lang's me arrrm.

Ignoring the question of why on earth anyone would want to write a poem to a glorified pile of tripe in the first place, what he means is this:

> Good luck to you and your honest, plump face
> Great chieftain of the pudding race!
> Above them all you take your place,
> Gut, stomach lining or intestine
> You are well worth a grace
> As long as my arm.

Which raises the question: why couldn't he just say that in the first place? The reason, I believe, is that the Scots do not want us to understand what they are saying. So, although an independent Scotland will be taking the English language with them, without us to translate for them they will have to start learning it properly if the rest of the world is going to understand anything they are saying.

If the English language made any sense, a catastrophe would be an apostrophe with fur.

Doug Larson

English, a language that lurks in dark alleys, beats up other languages and rifles in their pockets for spare vocabulary

Urban Dictionary

HOW THEY SAY 'ENGLISH' AROUND THE WORLD

France – Les Rosbifs: the 'roast beefs'. A Gallic commentary on the national cuisine, not just the sunburn.

Malaysia – Mat Salleh: 'mad sailor'. The crews of English sailing ships got pickled as newts in port and the name has stuck.

Roman Empire – Brittunculus: translates from Latin as 'wretched little Brit'.

South Africa – Soutie: from soutpiel, meaning 'salt penis' in Afrikaans. The idea is that the English have one leg in South Africa and one leg in England, leaving a certain appendage dangling in the brine . . .

America – English are called 'Limeys' since Royal Navy rations included limes to prevent scurvy. However, they could have been 'Krauts', as Captain Cook tried them on sauerkraut first but his men refused to eat it.

(NB Cockney rhyming slang for a Scot is 'sweaty': 'sweaty sock' = 'Jock'.)

[The English] have a lot of trouble with pronunciation, because they can't move their jaw muscles, because of malnutrition caused by wisely refusing to eat English food, much of which was designed and manufactured in medieval times during the reign of King Walter the Mildly Disturbed.

Dave Barry, *Dave Barry Talks Back*

A cut glass English accent can fool unsuspecting Americans into detecting a brilliance that isn't there.

Stephen Fry

4
A Short History of Anglo–Scots Rivalry

There's something about this referendum that feels a little bit like marriage counselling. Scotland: the flighty wife, tired of always being the butt of jokes at dinner parties, never getting to watch what she wants on the telly, never getting the spotlight, thinks she's outgrown old reliable England. 'You're boring', she claims, 'stuck in your ways. You never tell me how you feel. I want excitement, I want change, I want my independence back'. And we stand there, pretending to be shocked and hurt, but we can't lie; we've seen it coming for a while. We don't really care. We can't remember the last time we agreed on anything: football, politics, what constitutes a healthy, balanced diet. We're sick of all that deep-fried food she keeps cooking us, sick of her extravagant, rolling Rs, sick of hearing about Bannockburn *again*, every time she's had a bit too much to drink. Sitting there, on the therapist's couch, I want to recount the ups and downs of Anglo–Scots relations.

The earliest acknowledgement of tension between the cultured people of southern Albion and the warring barbarians from the Highlands came with the Romans, who built two huge walls to keep them apart: the Roman emperor Hadrian knocked up the first in AD 122 and then Antoninus Pius the second, which extended much deeper into Scotland, in AD 142. Traditionally these have been seen by historians as a desperate defence against the blue-faced barbarians they could never conquer; but it turns out that, actually, the north of England was just about as far as the Romans wanted to go. There was nothing to tempt them across the border. Fragments of letters have recently been discovered from Roman soldiers stationed on the walls – none of them mention nightmares of fearsome Scots, though one contains a desperate plea for more warm socks. Hadrian's Wall was never designed to prevent migration or to repel invaders, but was erected as a way of regulating and taxing imports. Scotland might like to brag – at the pub, pint of whisky in hand – about how fearsome its warriors were, but no legion was ever stationed at Hadrian's Wall; only customs soldiers.

Over the next thousand years things plodded along calmly enough. The Scots kept their hand in with a little light raiding of English cattle, but otherwise we coexisted like good neighbours (if good neighbours with a hefty fence between us). But their first really ambitious move was when Scots king Malcolm III challenged England's, that bastard William (sorry, I mean William the Bastard), in 1072. When William grumpily reached the Scottish borders, Malcolm (whose nickname was Big Head) employed the shrewd tactic of immediately surrendering. But it was all part of a cunning master plan to destabilise England. By 1075 William's own earls were revolting and within ten years he was dead.

After that our relationship was on rocky territory. Neither side trusted the other. If mobile phones had existed back then, you could bet that England would be sneaking a look at Scotland's texts every time she left the room. England's preferred enemy has always been the French, but spending every summer fighting in Normandy could drag. In 1296 Edward I clearly wanted a change and so he invaded Scotland and deposed King John. A certain William Wallace (so memorably and inaccurately captured in the tartan-clad blockbuster *Braveheart*), offered up some resistance at the Battle of Stirling Bridge, but the aptly named Hammer of the Scots soon had him hung out to dry – in five different locations.

In 1314 Robert the Bruce, one of Edward's trusted commanders, was sent north to police the Highlands. But he decided to change sides along the way. He surprised the Hammer's son, Edward II (sadly more of a spanner) at Bannockburn and, much to their surprise, the English were trounced. The first Parliament of Scotland met and, two years later, Edward III (more of a sledgehammer) signed the Treaty of Northampton, which recognised Scottish independence. But he was only joking and invaded the following year.

Scotland bided her time, grumbling to anyone who would listen about how mistreated she had been, and waited for the English to get distracted. When Henry VIII declared war on France in 1513, Scotland grabbed her moment and promptly invaded the north of England. This wasn't a success: they were promptly crushed at the Battle of Flodden Field and those few left alive limped home and continued plotting revenge.

Here's a name that pops up every time we fight: Mary, Queen of Scots. When Mary married the French dauphin in 1558 the English were alarmed: our two ancient Catholic enemies were uniting. But the French prince died young and Scotland's beautiful princess turned out more

Lindsey Lohan than Grace Kelly. Eventually she ran away from Edinburgh Castle and Elizabeth I's England was the only place that would take her in (and looked after her for twenty years). But, still unsatisfied with her comfy Yorkshire castle, Mary plotted revenge (unsuccessfully) against her cousin, Elizabeth, and was beheaded for treason. But she had the last laugh. When Elizabeth died childless in 1603, Mary's son James inherited the crown and Scotland and England were united (unsurprisingly, James left Scotland as soon as he could and never went back).

Unfortunately, England's new Scottish royal family proved neither steady nor popular. James' son Charles I, a Laurence Llewelyn-Bowen type of a king more famous for his flamboyantly ruffled collar than his parliamentary prowess, proved such a poor king that after a civil war that claimed around 200,000 lives, the English parliament tried him for treason and chopped his head off. The Stuarts got another chance with Charles II, but when he died without an heir and his very unpopular brother inherited the throne, England decided they'd rather have a Dutchman named after a fruit than another Scot.

England was in a reconciliatory mood, keen to patch things up, and so, in 1707, offered the political equivalent of a diamond ring: the Act of Union. We weren't just great, we were Great Britain.

Not everyone was happy with this and Scottish nationalists claimed the Scottish signatories were bribed. The poet Robert Burns later wrote: 'We are bought and sold for English gold. Such a parcel of rogues in a nation.'

In 1745 the last of the Stuarts, the self-styled Bonnie Prince Charlie, capitalised on Scottish anger about the

Act of Union and raised an army in the Highlands to claim the Scottish and English throne. But unfortunately for the Scots he wasn't much of a soldier and wimpishly stationed himself so far behind the battle lines that he couldn't actually see what a terrible mess he'd made of battle strategy. When his army met the English forces at Culloden they were completely crushed. Bonnie Prince Charlie escaped to Europe, dressed as a girl, leaving his supporters to face the extremely unpleasant consequences of their rebellion. Laws were passed condemning any man who wore a kilt to seven years in prison or transportation (this was the original crime against fashion). The English then began a brutal land-grab that became known as the Highland Clearances, an atrocity remembered by a ten-foot bronze statue in Sutherland and, less surprisingly, a urinal in a Glasgow pub bearing the names of those responsible so that customers can show their appreciation.

So, Scotland, you want to be your own country. Well, fair enough, but who are you going to turn to when things aren't going your way? That old historical ally, France? Spain perhaps? Maybe Ireland? That's a rhetorical question because we all know, don't we? Once she's had her fun – travelled the world, got a tattoo and spent all her money – she'll come back to us. And will we help her? The answer is probably yes, because that is the English way. Despite generations, or even centuries, of Scottish insults and attacks, she can rely on our support when she needs it. It's the small-island mentality that has repelled would-be invaders for thousands of years and built up a defensive mentality. It is why we do not learn other languages, are hostile to foreign tourists, will not listen to their music with any enjoyment and think their bathrooms are a disgrace.

Scotland, we know we've been harsh at times. We know we've been distracted, unfair and dismissive. But do you really want to call it quits? You still look great in that tartan skirt you always wear. Couldn't we put our differences aside and be great (Britain) again?

What enemy would invade Scotland, where there is nothing to be got?

Samuel Johnson

It's nae good blamin it oan the English fir colonising us. Ah don't hate the English. They're just wankers. We are colonised by wankers. We can't even pick a decent, vibrant, healthy culture to be colonised by. No. We're ruled by effete arseholes. What does that make us? The lowest of the fuckin low, tha's what, the scum of the earth. The most wretched, servile, miserable, pathetic trash that was ever shat intae creation. Ah don't hate the English. They just git oan wi the shite thuv goat. Ah hate the Scots.'

Renton in Irvine Welsh's *Trainspotting*

Edinburgh is the loft extension of England.

Al Murray

[On the Geordies] I love them. They're beautiful people. A genetically engineered race of hawklike people whose sole responsibility it is to keep the Scots out of England.

Al Murray

Asked by a Scot what Johnson thought of Scotland: 'That it is a very vile country, to be sure, Sir.' 'Well, Sir!' (replies the Scot, somewhat mortified), 'God made it.' Johnson: 'Certainly he did; but we must always remember that he made it for Scotchmen, and comparisons are odious, Mr. S------; but God made hell.'

Samuel Johnson

Braveheart is pure Australian shite . . . William Wallace was a spy, a thief, a blackmailer – a c**t basically. And people are swallowing it. It's part of a new Scottish racism, which I loathe – this thing that everything horrible is English. It's conducted by the great unread and the conceited w***ers at the SNP, those dreary little pr**ks in Parliament who rely on bigotry for support.

Billy Connolly

When he awoke it was dawn. Or something like dawn. The light was watery, dim and incomparably sad. Vast, grey, gloomy hills rose up all around them and in between the hills there was a wide expanse of black bog.

Stephen had never seen a landscape so calculated to reduce the onlooker to utter despair in an instant. 'This is one of your kingdoms, I suppose, sir?' he said. 'My kingdoms?' exclaimed the gentleman in surprise. 'Oh, no! This is Scotland!'

Susanna Clarke, Jonathan Strange & Mr Norrell

The noblest prospect which a Scotchman ever sees, is the high road that leads him to England!

Samuel Johnson

There was a Scotsman, an Englishman and Claudia Schiffer sitting together in a carriage in a train going through Wales. Suddenly the train went through a tunnel and as it was an old-style train, there were no lights in the carriages and it went completely dark. Then there was this kissing noise and the sound of a really loud slap. When the train came out of the tunnel, Claudia Schiffer and the Scotsman were sitting as if nothing had happened and the Englishman had his hand against his face as if he had been slapped.

The Englishman was thinking: 'The Scottish fella must have kissed Claudia Schiffer and she missed him and slapped me instead.'

Claudia Schiffer was thinking: 'The English fella must have tried to kiss me and actually kissed the Scotsman and got slapped for it.'

And the Scotsman was thinking: 'This is great. The next time the train goes through a tunnel I'll make that kissing noise and slap that English b**tard again.'

5
Money: What a Load of Bankers!

As we've all been told, *money makes the world go around*, and therefore it's no surprise that it was the English who first issued banknotes – turning *money* into a form to *go around* for the very first time. Some observers north of the border are convinced that when the Bank of Scotland was formed in 1696, it was the first in Europe to issue banknotes, therefore paving the way for a new global financial system. However, as usual, the English beat them to it. In 1694, the Bank of England received a royal charter to issue notes in exchange for the equivalent of £1.2 million in deposits of security, namely gold, which was used to build a navy. Within ten years England was one of the world's financial powerhouses and an Act of Union with Scotland in 1707 put an end (at least officially) to the warring and squabbling that had been going on between the neighbours for almost six hundred years. Scotland, by then, was simply no longer able to compete with England in military terms and had to use English pounds to buy its whisky. By the time of the Union it would take twelve Scottish pounds to buy one of the real English versions.

Curious then that the whole English (and global) financial system has its roots connected with seafaring, which, of course, led to the worldwide rise of swashbuckling pirates on the high seas. In fact, governments encouraged greedy subjects to sail out and relieve other nations of galleons full of gold and other valuable treasures to bring back to Blighty. The industry was full of murderous, treacherous villains ready to exploit and cheat their way to great riches. I wish I could say things have completely changed on the high seas of finance these days! They don't fly the Jolly Roger in the City of London but we all know it's still there. (But before the Scots get all smug, there are two words to mention here: 'Fred' and 'Goodwin'.)

The English have possibly the world's worst track record as peddlers of financial misery, so it's hardly surprising that the subject of money has always been considered a vulgar one and that discretion is usually considered necessary. One doesn't talk about money, you know; and yet it is all we think about. Probably more than even sex – so that's at least every six seconds, according to some reliable surveys (although that seems conservative to me. And I'm sure Labour are just as bad).

Excluding the Ferrari-driving bankers, the English have always displayed modesty, but that is hardly surprising when one considers how, for centuries, we have acquired our money. Always ruthlessly and at somebody else's expense. In rhyming slang: bankers, the lot of us. The Scots, on the other hand, have always been regarded as 'financially responsible', as some would put it. Tight as two coats of paint, others might say. While it isn't fair to say that the kilt was designed without pockets for a reason, it is true that there are many tales of Scottish frugality; and perhaps so many of them were born in North America just to save on the fare.

The proud Scots still cling on tightly to their pound (as if they might have to spend it), which is now equal in value to the English version, and the Bank of Scotland still issues them. The only problem is that they are not legal tender. Not even in Scotland. It is true that most English shopkeepers will accept them with grace, and most banks will allow accounts to be credited by using them. For the moment. The question is 'What will the Scots do if they vote themselves independent of England and the rest of the United Kingdom?' So what are their options? They could certainly issue their own currency, and even call it the Scottish Pound and make it legal in Scotland. But what would the value of that be against the real pound? Twelve to one as it was at the time of the Union, or far less than that? And would it be legal tender in England? (Answers on a postcard please.) Would it be accepted in Europe? (no need to answer that question) and what would it be called? The Scottish Pound? Or will it be called, with all the egos at work up in Scotland at the moment, the Salmond Pound? Whatever it is, if it does end up being worth twelve times less than the English Pound then I am definitely moving to Scotland next year.

To get off scot-free means to have escaped punishment and avoided the consequences of a bad deed. The origin of the phrase is traceable to Scandinavia (*not* Scotland, as it would appear) and the word 'scot', meaning 'payment'. Around the thirteenth century a great muni-cipal tax called 'scot' was imposed on the Scandinavian people. All households were required to pay according to their means, although peasants were exempt and thus 'scot-free'. In England the Scot Tax lasted in some places for hundreds of years, finally petering out during the Westminster electoral reforms of 1836. It is also known that during the Middle Ages, innkeepers would hold a record of a person's drinking on a slate called a scot and to leave an establishment without paying was known as 'going scot-free'. Remember that the next time a Scot fails to buy the next round.

My folks were English . . . we were too poor to be British.

Bob Hope, *My Life in Jokes*

England is a nation of shopkeepers.

Napoleon

In all four corners of the earth, one of these three names is given to him who steals from his neighbour: brigand, robber or Englishman.

Les Triades des Anglais (1572)

[In a Scottish accent] 'We don't need your English bastard pounds! We're our own country, we'll have our own bloody money, eh?!' [English accent] 'Would you like your own currency?' [Scottish accent] 'Ah, it's complicated mathematically. Let's just have yours with our photos, I think that's the best way!'

Michael McIntyre

The maxim of the British people is 'Business as usual.'

Winston Churchill

I know why the sun never sets on the British Empire: God would never trust an Englishman in the dark.

Duncan Spaeth

6
Cultured Pearls

England and Scotland have been interlinked culturally since long before 1707. But by the 1760s Scotland had so little literature of note that there was huge excitement when James McPherson discovered the works of an ancient Scottish epic poet. The *Lays of Ossian* were promptly translated into all the major languages of Europe. The only problem was that McPherson was cashing in on our hope that Scots could have as interesting and varied a culture as English did and the *Lays of Ossian* turned out to be a fake (unfortunately he'd already been buried among the English literary giants in London's Westminster Abbey before word got out). Undaunted by this, we've remained very hopeful about Scottish culture ever since. I could run through a long list of influential writers and thinkers: Robert Burns, Robert Louis Stevenson, Alexander McCall Smith – but they are far too easily trumped by the sheer box-office draw of England's William Shakespeare, Geoffrey Chaucer, Jane Austen and (ahem) E. L. James. (We are very good at high *and* low culture: see the Love and Sex chapter for more on this.) The two most famous Scottish novels are Sir Walter Scott's *Rob Roy*, which is virtually unreadable – Oh, come on. How many of you have actually read it? I have. *Rob Roy* is about an Englishman who has to travel to the Highlands to recover money stolen from his father by a thieving Scotsman, which says it all – and Irving Welsh's

Trainspotting, which is an all too convincing tale of drugs and violence on those Scottish housing estates the Japanese are warned about . . .

But when it comes to culture, we really are better together. Take Samuel Johnson, the English dictionary-writer, committed enemy of everything Caledonian and the one who noticed that McPherson was a fake – without his Scottish friend and biographer James Boswell faithfully transcribing his merciless quips (many of which are scattered throughout this book) and bringing him to life, today Johnson might be a minor footnote in our cultural history. Take James Bond, England's favourite fictional spy. He's been played by actors from every part of the United Kingdom but best by a Scottish nationalist. Take Robert Burns. He really is better, not to mention *understandable,* translated into English . . .

I love books but to me, culture is music. And since the 1960s England has been at the front and centre of the world's music industry. For over fifty years our musicians and artists have dominated the business and home-grown bands such as the Rolling Stones, Radiohead, the Who, Pink Floyd, Oasis and far too many more to list here have exported English culture around the world by the shipful. Scotland, on the other hand, hasn't. It's true that over the years they have produced some fine folk artists such as Donovan and . . . I can't think of any others – but it's not quite the same thing, is it? And before you start writing to me from Scotland about the Bay City Rollers, the Proclaimers and those poodle-haired poppers from the 1980s, Simple Minds, well, it's still not quite the same thing is it? Nor is Nazareth, Midge Ure or Annie Lennox when put on the same billboard as the Beatles and David Bowie and Paul Weller. There are reasons that the Scottish Tourist Board uses Travis's 'Why Does It Always Rain on Me?' in their adverts and it's not because it's a good song . . .

Still it is not all doom and gloom north of the border. They do have some wonderful bagpipe players, accordion music and a host of fine fiddlers. The harp, I am reliably informed, dates as far back as the Iron Age and lyres found on the Isle of Skye have been carbon dated to around 2300 BC. That's over four thousand three hundred years old! So while there is no doubt that Scotland is steeped in musical history, the only mystery is, with that long to practise, why Scotland has not ended up being rather better at it. It is England, and in particular London, where young and hopeful artists cut their teeth and hope to be noticed. But, despite Scottish independence that will not change. London has long welcomed all ages, colours, cultures, accents, fashions and fads. London has long lent an edge and a polish to the artistic skills of people from elsewhere: tartan was never cool until Vivienne Westwood and Malcolm McLaren made punk bondage trousers out of it. You will all still be welcome to travel south and try your luck in our great capital. There are plenty of places to play and to find work. Who am I trying to kid? It doesn't matter what colour, culture, accent, fashion or fad you have. If you are going to make the business folk of old London town money then you are welcome. If not, then save your train fare and concentrate on improving your bagpipe playing. There is a big demand around Hogmanay for the pipe players . . .

In 1975, Alex Mitchell of King's Lynn died of laughter while watching a kilted Scotsman using bagpipes to do battle against a black pudding. Laughing can kill: from cardiac arrest or asphyxiation due to loss of muscle-tone control.

'Why Does It Always Rain on Me?' was inspired by the misery of growing up in Glasgow. When Travis started to perform this song at the 1999 Glastonbury Festival, after being sunny for several hours, it began to rain exactly as the first line was sung.

He would not allow Scotland to derive any credit from Lord Mansfield; for he was educated in England. 'Much,' said he, 'may be made of a Scotchman, if he be caught young.'

James Boswell, speech in the House of Commons, 1828

In England only uneducated people show off their knowledge; nobody quotes Latin or Greek authors in the course of conversation, unless he has never read them.

George Mikes

7
Sport: We're All British (If You're Winning)

Since we've stopped rushing into battle and inflicting violent punishments on one another, the great skirmishes between England and Scotland have all centred on sport (although some sporting displays bear a striking resemblance to our earlier medieval scuffles). Nobody else in the world could care less but to the English and Scots there is no greater passion shown, or nationalist instinct displayed, than when they are playing rugby or football against each other. This would be true of cricket too, if anyone in Scotland could play the game. But they do have the Highland Games so they can toss tree trunks around instead. There has been the odd Scottish sporting icon over recent decades, such as Jim Clark and David Coulthard in motor racing, Colin Montgomerie in golf and Andy Murray in bat and ball, but when they are on television they are rightly regarded, south of the border, as British when they look like winning and Scottish when they lose. Now to the uninitiated this might sound unfair, and in fact it is unfair. But an independent Scotland would take all of Andy Murray's major triumphs (which amount to two) away from the English fans of rackets and would also deprive us of all Colin Montgomerie and David Coulthard's major victories, which are . . . erm, OK, let's move on.

The English are often criticised for never winning

anything important and to some extent this is a fair point. But, at least the English compete against the world, at some level, in almost every game going (and we did *invent* most of the world's most popular sports, so really we're just being modest when we let other teams win). Where, for example, are the great Scottish cricketers and their thrilling matches against Australia? Hands up any Welsh motor racing drivers, or teams. It certainly doesn't look like shinty, dancing around swords or throwing a sack of straw over a wall are going to become international sports any time soon.

So what happens when we do meet? In 1961, at Wembley, the Scottish football team were annihilated by the English, suffering a crushing defeat of 9–3. As the final whistle blew, the goalkeeper, Frank Haffey, was reduced to tears. He emigrated to Australia and never played for Scotland again.

But when we do let the Scots beat us, things get even more out of hand. The 1977 England v. Scotland match is memorable not for what happened during the game itself but for what happened on the pitch *after* the game. The Scottish fans, overcome with revolutionary spirit (and booze), ran onto the pitch, ripping up large sections of the grass and tearing down the goalposts. And thus football hooliganism was born (you can have that one, Scotland, it's all yours).

In 1996 our two teams took to the pitch again, each desperate for glory. England were in the lead for most of the match until, with fifteen minutes to go, Scotland were given a penalty. But the England goalkeeper managed, miraculously, to save it so that Paul Gascoigne, aka Gazza, could go on to score the winning goal. Was it superior skill on the part of the English team? Apparently not, according to self-proclaimed psychic and spoon-bender Uri Geller, who was hovering over the stadium in a helicopter at that precise moment. 'When that penalty kick was taken I willed Dave to dive to the right, and he did. And I willed the ball to move with pure telepathy.' Uri claimed that he had 'tapped into the massive wave of positive vibrations from the England supporters and beamed them down to the players'. All sounds a bit *Star Trek* to me.

If Scotland vote for independence, there will be little change in the spirit of our sporting encounters – we certainly won't let old acquaintance be forgot. And although the Welsh, and to a lesser extent the Irish, like to get in on the rivalry whenever England play them in any sport, it never really reaches the level of frenzy the Scots whip themselves into when one of their own scores a try or a goal against England. But, I suppose that is where seven hundred years of oppression gets you. At least they are no longer throwing sharpened sticks at us over the Wall.

Recently a Syrian international playing for a Scottish football team phoned home to speak to his mother. 'It's terrible here,' she told him. 'Your father has been shot at, your younger brother has joined a rebel gang and your sister is afraid to even leave the house. There is no fresh bread or clean water. And what's more,' she continued, 'it's your fault.'

'How?' he asked her.

'Because if it wasn't for you we wouldn't even be in Glasgow.'

Barmy Army is a phrase used to describe a rowdy group of people, usually sports fans, who are excitable, volatile and crazy. Barm is the froth produced by fermenting alcohol and in English prisons, inmates used to feign madness by 'putting on the barmy stick' (frothing at the mouth). In 1912 Fred Murray wrote and published a popular song that includes the line 'Ginger you're barmy, why don't you join the army', which formed part of a popular limerick during World War One when the line 'You'll get knocked out by a bottle of stout, Ginger you're barmy' was added. In 1994 rowdy English cricket fans who had followed the English team to Australia for the Ashes Tour were affectionately nicknamed the Barmy Army, an obvious equivalent of Scotland's football-fan Tartan Army.

The Englishman's love affair with golf is well-known. Their love affairs with women? Not so much. 'An Englishman is on the green of a golf course about to take a putt. Suddenly, a funeral procession passes. The Englishman raises his hat as the cortege passes as if in deep reflection. 'I never knew you were such a gentleman!' exclaimed his playing partner, to which the Englishman responds, 'Well, we were married for forty years!'

Rugby World Cup semi-final in 1991: Scotland had one of the strongest teams in the championship and had arguably their best ever chance of winning the World Cup. However, Gavin Hastings missed a penalty and England held on to win the match (incidentally, that was the furthest Scotland have got in the Rugby World Cup to this day).

Biggest winning margin for England v. Scotland in rugby: 43–3 (2001 Six Nations).

Calcutta Cup: out of all the occasions this has been played for (since 1879), England have won 55% of the time (Scotland have won 33% and 12% have ended in a draw).

Ping-pong was invented on the dining tables of England in the nineteenth century, and it was called wiff-waff. And there, I think, you have the difference between us and the rest of the world. Other nations, the French, looked at a dining table and saw an opportunity to have dinner; we looked at it and saw an opportunity to play wiff-waff.

Boris Johnson

Mortar fire is to be preferred, of course, to British sports fans.

P. J. O'Rourke

You say Bannockburn, I say Culloden, because it's not the heats that counts, it's the final. And you lot have never been in the final, have you?

Al Murray

Being an England supporter is like being the over-optimistic parents of the fat kid on sports day.

John Bishop

The reason why Englishmen are the best husbands in the world is because they want to be faithful. A Frenchman or an Italian will wake up in the morning and wonder what girl he will meet. An Englishman wakes up and wonders what the cricket score is.

Barbara Cartland

8

Food and Drink: The Full English Menu

Actor Mike Myers has a theory about Scotland's cuisine: it's all based on a dare. Case in point: haggis, the culinary equivalent of the dirty pint*, a delightful concoction of the heart, lungs and liver of some poor, unsuspecting sheep, minced with onion, oatmeal and suet and stuffed into the stomach lining of said sheep, made popular when Robert Burns declared that anyone who didn't eat it was a sissy, and the blue-faced warriors from across the border obediently grabbed their forks. The only place you'll find a dish similarly stomach-churning is France, in a fragrant little dish called *andouillette*, but, let's face it, the French will eat anything; you don't even have to dare them.

English cuisine, on the other hand, is less likely to challenge your gag reflex (except in the case of jellied eels – those crazy Cockneys will try to flog just about anything). In fact, there are plenty of treats to tickle your taste buds, and the common accusation that the English cannot cook seems rather unjust when you consider that England now boasts no fewer than four Three Michelin Star chefs. Scotland, unsurprisingly, has none.

Let us follow the Englishman, then, as he embarks on his culinary day.

---

* Pint glass filled with all the most disgusting shots the bar has to offer, mixed with half a pint of bitter. Usually drunk as a dare.

Starting the morning right means one thing: a full English breakfast. Flying the flag in luxury hotels and greasy spoons around the world, the full English (or fry-up) is a truly British dish. Each part of our proud nation has their own version: the Irish add soda bread; the Welsh go for laver bread; the Scots thought it needed a bit more blood and promptly ruined it by adding offal, but that's up to them. The dish's powers to revive are legendary – the scent of bacon sizzling away in a pan is enough alone to rouse our Englishman from the heaviest of alcohol-induced slumbers, and right him for the day ahead.

After this hefty meal, the Englishman needs something a little lighter to bridge the gap between breakfast and dinner, and the most English of lunches is, of course, the sandwich. The story of its invention is legendary. John Montague, fourth Earl of Sandwich, was gambling into the early hours when he decided that he needed a snack. Not wanting to get greasy fingerprints all over his cards, thus giving himself a tactical disadvantage, he ordered his servants to bring him meat between two slices of bread. It was an instant hit. Montague himself was not so popular, and was thought to be a member of the notorious Hellfire Club (a gentlemen's society set up to ridicule religion, rumoured to be rife with orgies and satanic rituals). Not as innocent as it seems, that sandwich. Over the years we English have created a variety of sandwich classics, from the honest, working-class cheese and pickle to the rather effete cucumber sandwich favoured by the upper classes in Victorian England.

Come four o'clock, the Englishman needs an excuse for a sit-down. 'There are few hours in life more agreeable,' notes Henry James, 'than the hour dedicated to the ceremony known as afternoon tea.' The relationship between the English and their tea is one so intense, so passionate, that it's hard to imagine the two could ever exist without one another. The origins of tea are more exotic than our shores. One early legend, dating back nearly five thousand years, is that it was the Buddhist monk Bodhidharma who discovered tea. Apparently he had fallen asleep while meditating and didn't wake for nine years. When he did finally come round, he immediately sliced off his eyelids as self-punishment for his idleness. When he cast them away, they took root in the soil and grew into tea bushes. In England, tea-drinking became fashionable with the arrival of the Portuguese princess Catherine of Braganza, who married Charles II in 1662, and became even more popular when Princess Anne decided to ditch her morning glass of ale in favour of a nice brew. Quickly, the English made it their own, adding milk and making a bit of a song and dance about it by inventing afternoon tea. Now no longer the preserve of the upper classes, the humble cuppa sits comfortably on any table, from the Ritz to the building site (though the latter, 'builders' brew', might contain a few more sugars).

It has reached the time of day when the Englishman must decide what to have for dinner. There are a number of English classics on offer: bangers and mash, shepherd's pie, a Sunday roast, toad in the hole, chicken tikka masala (invented in Birmingham). But it's Friday and so fish and chips is the order of the day, with a splash of H.P. (that's short for Houses of Parliament) Sauce on the side. A reminder of a time when we were a little more religious and refrained from meat between Friday and Sunday, to most people fish Fridays mark a celebration of the end of the working week and the queues outside the chippie on a Friday evening remain as long as ever. During the Second World War, fish and chips was judged so important to the national morale that it was one of the few foods to evade rationing.

Day done, it's time to retreat to the pub, but *not* for a warm beer. I don't know what to say about the misconception that the English drink warm beer because I have never drunk it and nor has anybody I know. Real ale, however, is brewed to be drunk at room temperature and should never be served straight from the freezer; if you want to put ice in your ale then that's your own business but I suggest you stick to cans of Tennent's Extra and leave English beer to our more refined palates.

But the best drink to mark the end of a day wherever you are – and one that always needs lots of ice – is a gin and tonic (the gin of course needs to be London Dry Gin). Originally nicknamed 'mother's ruin', in the eighteenth century gin was associated with seedy neighbourhoods and the lecherous working classes, who knocked it back like it was water and forgot all of their responsibilities in the process. In 1736, when high taxes were imposed that pushed up the price, there were riots on the streets. However, it is now sipped sophisticatedly by the middle classes in wine bars and at dinner parties amid conversation about how little Millicent did in her Latin exams. The quinine that gives tonic water its characteristic tang was, until recently, the only cure for malaria; tonic water was invented by English expats in the far-flung parts of the Empire in the nineteenth century as a civilised way of getting their daily protection against the disease. Trust the English to turn bitter medicine into a cocktail that everyone wants to drink.

The former French president Jacques Chirac once said of the English, 'One cannot trust people whose cuisine is so bad,' to which I have one response: how come London is now France's fourth biggest city? Even Michel Roux is English. As for Scotland, a country where a bag of chips is considered salad and a deep-fried Mars Bar is a Friday-night delicacy, they can keep their Scotch eggs, we're not mad on them and they're ginger anyway. And I'm with Samuel Johnson on *oat cuisine* – it's strictly for the horses.

There is a feeling which persists in England that making a sandwich interesting, attractive, or in any way pleasant to eat is something sinful that only foreigners do.

Douglas Adams

The English contribution to world cuisine – the chip.

John Cleese

I'm on a whisky diet. I've lost three days already.

Tommy Cooper

I went to a restaurant that serves 'breakfast at any time'. So I ordered French toast during the Renaissance.

Peter Kay

Bacon and eggs walk into a bar. The bartender takes one look at them and says:

'Sorry, we don't serve breakfast.'

[To Mr Arthur Lee mentioning some Scotch who had taken possession of a barren part of America, and wondering why they would choose it.]

Johnson: 'Why, Sir, all barrenness is comparative. The Scotch would not know it to be barren.' Boswell: 'Come, come, he is flattering the English. You have now been in Scotland, Sir, and say if you did not see meat and drink enough there.' Johnson: 'Why yes, Sir; meat and drink enough to give the inhabitants sufficient strength to run away from home.'

On the continent people have good food; in England people have good manners.

George Mikes

I realised why the English are big tea drinkers. Just taste their coffee and you'll see the reason.

Joey Adams

Britain is the only country in the world where the food is more dangerous than the sex.

Jackie Mason

The British have an umbilical cord which has never been cut and through which tea flows constantly. It is curious to watch them in times of sudden horror, tragedy or disaster. The pulse stops apparently, and nothing can be done, and no move made, until 'a nice cup of tea' is quickly made. What a pity all countries are not so tea-conscious. World peace conferences would run more smoothly if 'a nice cup of tea', or indeed, a samovar were available at the proper time.

Marlene Dietrich

ITEMS OF FOOD TAKEN BY THE QUEEN WHEN SHE GOES ABROAD

Harrods sausages
Mint sauce
Jam
Barley sugar
Malvern water
Shortbread
China and Indian tea
Fruit cake

My wife and I tried two or three times in the last forty years to have breakfast together, but it was so disagreeable we had to stop.

Winston Churchill

To eat well in England, you should have breakfast three times a day.

W. Somerset Maugham

In England there are sixty different religions, and only one sauce.

Domenico Caracciola, Neopolitan diplomat

England and the English as a rule, they will refuse even to sample a foreign dish, they regard such things as garlic and olive oil with disgust, life is unlivable to them unless they have tea and puddings.

George Orwell

England manufactures most of the world's airline food, as well as all the food you ever ate in your junior-high-school cafeteria.

Dave Barry

My girlfriend bought a cookbook the other day called *Cheap and Easy Vegetarian Cooking*. Which is perfect for her, because not only is she vegetarian . . .

Jimmy Carr

I had a ploughman's lunch the other day. He wasn't very happy.

Tommy Cooper

9
Weather: 'In Hertford, Hereford and Hampshire Hurricanes Hardly Happen'

Samuel Johnson once claimed that 'when two Englishmen meet, their first talk is of the weather.' It's inevitable; we can barely stop ourselves from doing it. In *Watching the English* Kate Fox suggests that 'Nice April we're having' or 'Where did *that* downpour come from?' are really just English code for 'I'd like to talk to you, will you talk to me?' (which makes us sound like a country full of quivering librarian types, lingering in public spaces ready to pounce on unsuspecting passers-by). Nevertheless, I take it as a warning sign. Whenever I am overseas and somebody who is obviously either English or Scottish (you can tell by the sunburn), attempting small talk, starts a conversation with some comment about the weather, I put on my best foreign accent and say, 'Eh, sorry but I don't speak the good English' and move on. Of course, the other way to throw someone off is to disagree, the ultimate social faux pas in weather-talk; or, if you are *actually* foreign, to enter into weather-based one-upmanship (we English hate it when you throw your much more thrilling weather in our faces).

But it is easy to see why the English are obsessed with the weather. After all, we live in a country without real extremes. It is neither tropical nor polar. Thanks to the Gulf Stream, England has a temperate climate and, while parts of the south coast can occasionally feel Mediterranean, it is never Saharan. While it may snow from time to time, it's never landscape-altering like it is in Moscow or Newfoundland, two places on roughly the same latitude as England. Perhaps that is why we are never prepared for extreme weather. The English are used to their trains being cancelled in winter because of the 'wrong kind of snow' and accept it with a tut as an inevitability, though it's hard to imagine National Rail ever declaring that they are currently experiencing uninterrupted punctuality across their services thanks to 'the right kind of snow'. We laugh along with our weather forecasters when they make jokes about how unlikely it is that a hurricane is on the way and then the biggest storm in forty years blasts the south-east.

Why the English talk about the weather so much is because it changes so quickly, though admittedly it is not as bad as in some parts of Scotland, where it can be all beautiful, calm and serene one moment and then go mad the next (not unlike their women). We care about our gardens, *do* wash our cars and *don't* want to get caught in the rain that can come at any moment, even on a fine day. In Scotland rain is a given, so nobody needs to talk about the weather. And it is another common mistake to assume that it is *always* raining in England. In fact England comes in at number 46 on the list of annual rainfall statistics – which, out of 200 countries including Africa and the Middle East where it never rains, is quite good going. Even America and New Zealand have higher rainfall figures. As for Scotland? Take your Wellington boots, that's all I am saying. They didn't invent the mackintosh up there without reason.

And the unpredictability of our weather is no bad thing, on some occasions. In 1588 Sir Francis Drake was playing bowls on a calm summer's day in August when the Spanish Armada appeared off the English coast. Much has been made of the Royal Navy's ruthless destruction of the fleet and forces that far outnumbered them but it was, in fact, our weather that prevented them reaching the shore. The wind picked up and turned against them, scattering the fleet. The English, with the wind in their favour, had a huge advantage and in the end an unexpected storm shipwrecked the Armada along the rocky southern coast of Ireland. (Drake later claimed that it wasn't the weather that stopped him from rushing into battle, but the fact that he was so unfazed by the Spanish that he waited to finish his bowls game before strolling off to defeat them). The same could be said of the D-Day landings in 1944, when the German command simply failed to expect an Allied assault because the weather was so terrible. They were so confident that nothing was going to happen that many of them were even on leave as the landings began. The Germans' fatal mistake was to overlook our hard-won ability (honed over a lifetime of experiencing four seasons in a single day) to make the best out of whatever hand our weather had dealt out.

On the other hand, unpredictability led to the rise of that ugliest of industries: the package holiday. As the post-war generation grew up during the 1950s and 60s they were no longer attracted by the Scottish Tourist Board's offer of gentle walks amongst the rainswept heather and the chance of spotting mysterious monsters in lochs. The English wanted their sunshine guaranteed and they wanted lager, lots of it. And so we all packed ourselves off to southern Spain, where we would be guaranteed fourteen days of uninterrupted, glorious sunshine during July and August each year. The Spanish coastline was transformed during those years into an unsightly spread of concrete hotels and bars, much to the relief of everybody living in Cornwall where the weather is equally reliable but the scenery infinitely more beautiful; if it wasn't for Frank Whittle inventing the turbojet engine then southern Cornwall would now look like Torremolinos (thanks Frank, you're a true English hero). We've had a lot of fun learning how to shout in English with a Spanish accent at waiters and barmen (the closest many of us are going to get to learning a new language), insisting on washing down full English breakfasts, roast dinners and fish and chips with as much cheap sangria as we could get down our necks, and returning home with sunstroke and shredded livers. Ah the English weather: if it wasn't so unpredictable then none of that would ever have happened.

Mad dogs and Englishmen go out in the midday sun.
Noel Coward

It was so cold the politicians had their hands in their own pockets.

Bob Hope

Fog in Channel – Continent cut off.
English newspaper headline

Conversation about the weather is the last refuge of the unimaginative.

Oscar Wilde

To an outsider, the most striking thing about the English weather is that there is not very much of it. All those phenomena that elsewhere give nature an edge of excitement, unpredictability and danger – tornadoes, monsoons, raging blizzards, run-for-your-life hailstorms – are almost wholly unknown in the British Isles.

Bill Bryson

You must never contradict anyone when discussing the weather.

George Mikes

ARCHAIC ENGLISH WORDS TO DESCRIBE BAD WEATHER (enough to trump any conversation)

PORT-BOYS small white clouds in a clear sky
WINDOGS white clouds blown by the wind
EDDENBITE a mass of cloud in the form of a loop
SLATCH a brief respite or interval in the weather
SWALLOCKY sultry weather
SHUCKY unsettled weather
TRUGGY dirty weather
EGGER-NOGGER sleet
SMITHER DIDDLES bright spots on either side of
   the sun

10
Love and Sex: Lie Back and Think of England

The scenario is tediously familiar from countless romcoms. English bachelor trips into the path of American or otherwise foreign beauty, with whom he is instantly and hopelessly besotted, and he must, despite his characteristically English awkwardness, find some way to win her heart. Bumbling his way through social encounters as gracelessly as a hippopotamus on roller skates, our floppy-haired Lothario, all teeth, chin and sense of propriety, is more likely to be found next to the buffet clutching his cucumber sandwiches, his glasses steaming up at the slightest mention of romantic encounter, than strutting his stuff on the dance floor.

And it is this stereotype that presents itself to the world, declaring the English to be a bunch of upper-middle-class buffoons who, in the face of, ahem, *sex*, are reduced to nothing but a whimper.

He is probably played by Colin Firth, or, preferably, Hugh Grant. But just as Hugh Grant's antics off-film are a far cry from his characters' (we all remember *that* little mess this particular heart-throb got himself into), we English aren't as buttoned-up as we are often cast. There's naughtiness lurking underneath our cardigans and novelty ties . . .

We are reserved, yes; keeping the details of our sex lives private is certainly an English characteristic – but why the hell not? I think everybody should. Who really wants to know about it anyway? But if we really *are* uptight, how come tabloid newspapers and magazines are incessantly revealing the detailed sex lives of very ordinary people, turning them into Z-list celebrities in the process? There must be a market for it here.

The common line is that while Mediterraneans have always been comfortable with things of a sexual nature, greeting strangers with a barrage of kisses and enthusiastically shedding clothes for a spot of communal sunbathing (indeed, archaelogists at Pompeii found several Roman comedy nightlights in the shape of winged penises) the English have always had a rather stiff approach to the matter (no pun intended). But our history tells a different story entirely, and is full of people behaving badly, from Nell Gwyn to Nelson and Lady Hamilton. Think Lady Godiva riding naked through Coventry in protest against her husband, the Earl of Mercia's, tax on the city (she couldn't have done that in Scotland, what with the weather up there). Or supposedly prudish Queen Victoria, who commissioned a 'private portrait' for her husband with a cheeky bit of shoulder on show. The Victorians might have covered the legs of the piano in case it incited lust, but this is far more revealing about their dirty minds than their sexual repression.

The notion that at the mere mention of intimacy or the prospect of bare flesh the English suddenly turn into a Jeeves and Wooster-style character, all shiny red faces and tittering behind the backs of hands, seems about as far removed from reality as the idea that *Fifty Shades of Grey* is well written (by its notably unabashed and un-buttoned-up English author). For that matter, have a look at our record in terms of literature, art and music. England has led the world in smut for centuries. Anyone who has picked through the glossary of their *Complete Shakespeare* will realise how filthy our Immortal Bard really was. *Harris' List of Covent Garden Ladies* was published in 1797: the first annual directory of working prostitutes. Most of our tabloids run pictures of topless women to this day. Our lap-dancing venues go under the euphemism of 'gentlemen's club' – but let's just say that none of their customers conform to any conventional concepts of how English gentlemen should behave. We even invented 'dogging'.

But still, we quite like to promote the idea that we are of a nervous disposition when it comes to sex. Perhaps it's Hugh Grant's fault: his awkward charm always wins him the girl in the end. Thankfully, we have the French as our scapegoats, and thus a snog is 'a French kiss' (as if the English would never have thought of anything more impassioned than a peck on the cheek), syphilis is 'the French disease', a condom is 'a French letter' and oral sex is 'the French style'. They are wise to us, though – the French name for sadomasochism is 'the English vice'. A Glasgow kiss, on the other hand, is a headbutt.

Continental people have sex lives; the English have hot-water bottles.

George Mikes

A plane crashes on a desert island. There are only a few survivors: three Spanish people, three French people and an Englishman. Six months later: one of the Spanish men has killed the other and is now living with the Spanish woman, the three French people have decided to become a threesome and the Englishman is still waiting to be introduced to the others.

I like the English. They have the most rigid code of immorality in the world.

Malcolm Bradbury

My girlfriend sat me down the other day for a chat. I say 'chat' – it was her talking at me for six hours. I didn't realise that when men say they're 'spoken for' that's actually what they mean. She said 'Jimmy, our relationship is at a crossroads. Down one road is struggle and hardship, but eventually, happiness. The other, well, that's a dead end.' So I replied, 'That's not a crossroads, that's a T-junction.'

Jimmy Carr

The air is soft and delicious. The men are sensible and intelligent. The English girls are divinely pretty and they have one custom which cannot be too much admired. When you go anywhere on a visit, the girls kiss you. They kiss you when you arrive. They kiss you when you go away. They kiss you when you return. Once you have tasted how soft and fragrant those lips are, you could spend your life there.

Desiderius Erasmus, *On England*

What a pity it is that we have no amusements in England but vice and religion!

Sydney Smith

My wife and I both made a list of five people we could sleep with. She read hers out and there were no surprises —1 George Clooney, 2 Brad Pitt etc. I thought 'I've got the better deal here' – 1 Your sister . . .

Michael McIntyre

I like threesomes with two women, not because I'm a cynical sexual predator. Oh no! But because I'm a romantic. I'm looking for 'The One'. And I'll find her more quickly if I audition two at a time.

Russell Brand

I I
A History of Britain in
Twenty-Six Objects

We've talked a lot about history, sport, language and literature, about weather and sex. But what *objects* leap to mind when you think of Scotland and how genuinely Scottish are they? Haggis? No, that's an English import. What about the kilt? Surely that's a Scottish uniform of sorts – although, as Ambrose Bierce pointed out, it's one that tends to be worn only by Scots in America and Americans in Scotland. But my research shows that kilts turn out to be Scandinavian, only arriving in the Highlands during the seventeenth century. So that's William Wallace and Robert the Bruce off the list of proud kilt owners. And as for tartan where each clan is distinguished by their own special version, that's only been around since the mid-nineteenth century when it was created by Victorians keen to knock up a more picturesque history for Scotland.

What about castles? Well, Balmoral could be seen as quite Scottish, apart from the fact it was bought by a German for an English queen. The Loch Ness Monster would definitely be Scottish, if such a beast existed. The Forth Bridge is certainly an iconic Scottish landmark, but it was designed and built by the English engineers Sir Benjamin Baker and Sir John Fowler. They were brought in after the previous attempt to cross the water ended in disaster in 1879 when the Scottish-built Tay Suspension Bridge collapsed, killing seventy-five people. The unicorn is a Scottish icon and the nation's official animal, which would be fine if it actually existed; and the greatest piece of theatre in history, known worldwide as 'The Scottish Play' (*Macbeth*), was actually written by the English genius William Shakespeare.

Turning your gaze to England, there is an equally confusing array of historic and iconic imagery ranging from red telephone boxes to policeman's helmets and the Archbishop of Canterbury, none of which are of any use any more. Black taxis, afternoon tea, bowler hats, polished shoes and umbrellas all feel as English as they come. As do the class system and queues. Big Ben, Stonehenge, St Paul's Cathedral and Tower Bridge are all images that represent England to the rest of the world on tea towels and biscuit tins, and England plc. has been making damn sure that sentiment doesn't get in the way of squeezing the maximum amount of profit out of them. You've got to pay to go into St Paul's today. Druids are no longer allowed near Stonehenge to celebrate the summer solstice in case they damage this valuable tourist site. And one of our proudest stories is of the American billionaire who discovered, after paying a fortune to ship it across the world and then painstakingly reconstructing it block by block in Arizona, that he'd bought London Bridge, not Tower Bridge. Caveat emptor – let the buyer beware. The English are every bit as canny as the Scots.

The objects that really sum up our different nations are our flags. The Scots have the saltire: a white cross on a blue background. The story goes that, in AD 832, King

Angus opportunistically invaded Northumbria and, when he found himself surrounded by a larger English army, he prayed for help. Seeing a cloud forming a white cross against the blue sky (the symbol of St Andrew), he vowed that if he won victory, Andrew would thereafter be the patron saint of Scotland. So even their flag tells a tale of another bloody defeat of England against the odds – with a bit of divine intervention. We don't have such a neat story about ours. The red cross of St George has been England's symbol since Richard the Lionheart took it on the Crusades with him and it has flown proudly on battlefields, newly discovered lands and out of the windows of our council estates ever since. To be completely honest, many of us are a bit embarrassed by it. What we much prefer is our joint flag – the Union Jack – where the white saltire of St Andrew, the red saltire of Ireland's St Patrick and the red cross of St George all sit happily together. No law has been passed making the Union Jack the national flag of the United Kingdom: it has simply become one through precedent. So we don't need a flag to proclaim who we are but, trust me, we really are better together.

He was inordinately proud of England and he abused her incessantly.

H.G. Wells

It was always yet the trick of our English nation, if they have a good thing to make it too common.

William Shakespeare

At dinner, Mrs Thrale expressed a wish to go and see Scotland. Johnson: 'Seeing Scotland, Madam, is only seeing a worse England. It is seeing the flower gradually fade away to the naked stalk.'

Samuel Johnson

If England was what England seems,
An' not the England of our dreams,
But only putty, brass, an' paint,
'Ow quick we'd drop 'er! But she ain't!

Rudyard Kipling

The British are special. The world knows it. In our innermost thoughts we know it. This is the greatest nation on earth.

Tony Blair

Be Britain still to Britain true,
Amang oursels united;
For never but by British hands,
Maun British wrangs be righted.

Robert Burns

Quiz: How English Are You?

1. There is a fight going on in next-door's garden between two people from different countries. Do you:
   A: Call for calm
   B: Call the authorities
   C: Jump over two fences and join in?

2. You are checking in at an airport and there is a huge queue. Do you:
   A: Ignore the question – you're hungover and have overslept so you are not even there yet
   B: Push your way to the front to complain
   C: Queue patiently and worry about missing your flight?

3. You are on holiday and notice that the hotel pool bar opens at 8 a.m. Do you:
   A: Think 'That's a bit early for a drink'
   B: Get stuck straight in
   C: Think 'I'll get in there after lunch'?

4. You are sitting outside a country pub when a game of cricket starts on the village green. Do you:
   A: Watch with mild interest for a while as you have lunch
   B: Think 'What a bunch of tossers'
   C: Settle in for the afternoon?

5. You are in a different city because your team is playing the local side. When the barman refuses to serve you, do you:

    A: Accept his decision and move on to another bar

    B: Start an argument as to your rights and his lack of respect

    C: Leave and throw a brick through the window?

6. What does the Statue of Lord Nelson in Trafalgar Square commemorate?

    A: The Battle of Trafalgar

    B: Something to do with Nelson Mandela

    C: The Battle of Trafalgar.

7. What is the highest peak in England?

    A: Scafell Pike

    B: Ben Nevis

    C: Who cares?

8. What drink is traditionally taken in the afternoons?

    A: Cold beer

    B: Tennent's Super Strength Lager

    C: Tea.

9. In which year did William of Orange invade England?

    A: 1789

    B: He can do it every year as far as I'm concerned

    C: He didn't invade, he was already English and was invited.

10. You see a badly sunburned young person at the airport. You hope they are:

A: Going to be OK

B: English

C: Scottish.

11. What is the best thing about Scotland?

A: The beautiful scenery and local hospitality

B: Aye, our city pubs and glorious history

C: The M74 to the M6 (Southbound).

12. What is the best thing about England?

A: Long sunny afternoons, riverside pubs and the culture

B: Scotland

C: Afternoon tea and cricket.

Answers
Mostly As: You are a relatively normal person
Mostly Bs: You are Scottish
Mostly Cs: You are definitely English.